*Painting by Minnesotans
of Norwegian Background
1870–1970*

This presentation is dedicated to my wife Lila
without whom I could do nothing

and to Harry and Josefa Andersen,
whose enthusiasm for Norwegian immigrant art
and whose support of the fine arts at Vesterheim
have long been an inspiration to me.

Painting by Minnesotans
of Norwegian Background
1870–1970

MARION JOHN NELSON

Special Publication
Norwegian-American Historical Association

This publication accompanies the Minnesota Historical Society exhibition *Painting by Minnesotans of Norwegian Background 1870–1970* showing at the James J. Hill House, St.Paul, March 31–October 16, 2000. A small companion publication, *Norwegian-American Painting in Minnesota Today* is being produced by the Groveland Gallery, Minneapolis, to accompany its exhibition of that name showing April 29–June 3, 2000. Sally Johnson is administrator and Claire Selkurt author and curator.

Front cover. Axel E. Schar. See pp. 42, 89.
          St. Louis County Historical Society
Back cover. Orabel Thortvedt. See pp.37–39, 93.
          Eva and Carl Hedstrom
Inside front and back covers and pages 4, 26, 28. Charles Thoresen.
          Sketchbooks. See pp. 37, 49, 92.
          Rosemari and Dennis Anderson
Page 2. Mathias Wolden. Sketchbook. See pages 44, 94.
          Tweed Museum of Art, UM Duluth, Gift of Gendron Jensen
Page 66. Magnus Norstad. Pen sketch (on letter to Louis W. Hill,
          November 4, 1917). See pages 50, 86. James J. Hill Reference
          Library, St. Paul.

Contents

Acknowledgments

I am deeply indebted to the Minnesota Historical Society for sponsoring the exhibition that forms the basis of this publication in connection with the conference *Vandringer: Norwegians in the American Mosaic, 1825–2000,* co-sponsored by the Society and the Norwegian-American Historical Association with John R. Christianson as Chair. I am also deeply indebted to the Association for assuming responsibility for the publication of this volume and to its Editor Odd S. Lovoll for writing the Introduction.

Staff members at the Minnesota Historical Society of special significance in planning and handling the details of the exhibition are former Curator of Art Thomas O'Sullivan, Hill House Site Manager Craig Johnson, and Assistant Registrar Nicole Delfino. Staff members of the Norwegian-American Historical Association who gave special assistance are its Administrative Director Kim Holland, Assistant Secretary Ruth Crane, and Copy Editor Mary Hove.

The publication would not have been possible without the financial support of the Ella and Kaare Nygaard Foundation, administered by St. Olaf College. This foundation also sponsored the restoration of the College's Herbjorn Gausta painting *The Secret* for inclusion in the exhibition.

My very special gratitude goes to the 28 lenders to the exhibition whose cooperation in it also made the works accessible for inclusion in this publication. The largest single lenders are Vesterheim, with twelve works, and the Minnesota Historical Society with six. Information supplied by these lenders on the artists and the works was also exceedingly helpful. That supplied by members of the artists' families is recognized in the sources for each artist given near the end of this volume.

Due to the nature of my approach, genealogical information on the artists was of special importance. Where that was not already part of the record or known by the artist's family,

the assistance of genealogist Lee Rokke, Apple Valley, MN, was invaluable.

Resource institutions of special significance were the Minneapolis Public Library, where JoEllen Haugo and others in the Special Collections were especially helpful; the Minneapolis Institute of Arts Library, where Mary D. McElroy Bass gave the project much individual attention; Vesterheim Museum Library, where Carol Hasvold was always ready to assist; the Norwegian-American Historical Association Archives, where Forrest Brown gave generously of his time and expertise; and the Minnesota Historical Society Library, where the work of Librarian Kay V. Spangler compiled under the title *Survey of Serial Fine Art Exhibitions and Artists in Minnesota, 1900–1970* (1997) is a resource on Minnesota art without equal. This work unfortunately did not become known to me until after much of my research had been completed, but it supplemented that substantially and gave me another source against which to check my information. Numerous outlying libraries were also helpful, of which the following deserve special mention: the Nobles County Library in Worthington, Minnesota; the Duluth Public Library; the Northeast Regional Historical Library, Duluth; and the Canton and Aberdeen public libraries in South Dakota.

I am grateful to Darrell Henning for his photography of works from Vesterheim, to Bruce Ojard and John Borge respectively for theirs of works at the St. Louis County Historical Society and the Moorhead Public Library, and to James Horns for his of works cleaned by him.

The friendly professional assistance and direction of Don Leeper, Elizabeth Cleveland and Donna Burch of Stanton Publication Services eased the pain of production.

Finally, I would be amiss in not mentioning my wife Lila, who entered the text on the computer and, with Mary Hove, assisted with the copy editing.

Introduction

Historical evidence must as a matter of simple logic encompass not only the traditional documents and manuscripts of scholarly inquiry but also the standard props of a material culture, from buildings to implements, clothing, ornaments, and monuments. In order to approach anything like historical reality, the concept of culture must consequently integrate the physical and intellectual worlds in a given period; a cultural refinement of thought, emotion, manners, taste, and belief gives expression to the fine arts, literary form, scholarly pursuits, and religious faith. These artifacts of the past—material and spiritual—provide cogent historical records.

The visual and physical remains of civilization naturally possess a greater public appeal than do musty documents, scrolls, and voluminous written works. Artistic portrayal, as well as literary art, responds to the sociocultural dynamics and vogues of its own time. In the Norwegian-American community authors of diverting literature and painters with esthetic sensitivity arrived relatively late on the scene. Works of fiction written in Norwegian appeared only in the mid-1870s, fifty years after the arrival of the first immigrants, but flourished for nearly seventy years thereafter. In their narratives the authors treated a wide range of subjects, focusing on the many aspects of ethnic life; the immigrant authors were amateurs who wrote about, and in general for, the immigrants themselves.

The gifted landscape painter John Olsen Hammerstad, who came to Chicago from Norway in 1869, is generally recognized as the first professional artist of Norwegian birth in the Midwest. The fine arts among Norwegian Americans developed from the following decade in metropolitan centers such as Chicago, Minneapolis, Brooklyn, and Seattle, as the Norwegian colonies there matured and developed urban cultures. Many painters were, like their literary contemporaries, amateurs, or at least did not make a living through their art; but a core of professional artists did emerge. Even these supplemented incomes in related professions, as illustrators and commercial artists, or even as housepainters. Their influence had a cultural impact far beyond the city. As an artistic elite in an ethnic urban world—a subject only relatively recently given systematic scholarly attention—they have rarely been properly recognized in general studies of Norwegian-American life. Most Norwegian Americans continued to reside outside large metropolitan areas. Nevertheless, an increase in the urban exodus from Norway, and a youth migration from Norwegian-American farming communities, made the urban colonies grow.

In the 1920s artists in Chicago and Brooklyn held juried commercial shows; these exhibitions made visible an urbane taste and revealed the artistic activity stimulated by the ethnic community. Norwegian practitioners of the fine arts in Minneapolis, with its Norwegian dominance, did not, as for instance in Chicago where Norwegians constituted a minority, form a closely knit group. Instead the artists interacted individually with the urban environment rather than separated as an organized artistic elite. Motifs from Norway occurred early and found a limited market among upwardly mobile Norwegian Americans. The immigrants themselves were seldom portrayed, although the landscapes in which they lived and worked were. Art was a commodity that appealed to middle-class consumer tastes in the Norwegian-American community; the relative prosperity of the 1920s encouraged artistic endeavor; markets, unlike those for literature in Norwegian, could be found both within and outside the Norwegian-American population. Artistic choices and genres pursued by artists of Norwegian extraction consequently reveal much about the dynamics of immigrant life and adjustment in the city.

Odd S. Lovoll
Editor
The Norwegian-American Historical Association

Author's Preface

This is not a study of culture in the Norwegian-American community. It is rather the study of Norwegians in the creative arts community of Minnesota. The selection of artists presented was not made by looking at who supplied the art for the Norwegian immigrants in Minnesota but who among the artists of Minnesota had their roots in Norway. This accounts for the specific wording of the title, *Painting by Minnesotans of Norwegian Background*.

The contribution or even character of immigrants is often looked for in their communities because in them the ethnic background can be taken for granted and the character and contributions are of a group nature that can be easily identified. A problem with this approach to immigrant studies is that with immigrants as near the culture they were entering as the Scandinavians were to the American, only a minority are found in close immigrant communities. The others are hard to track but they still have their place in the total picture of immigration. I have taken my approach in an attempt to deal with art among the hidden as well as the exposed Norwegians of Minnesota and to determine how these Norwegians who were concealed in the total fabric of the area subtly affected it.

The people included in this study are a non-scientific random sampling of Minnesota painters with Norwegian backgrounds arrived at through my experience as a life-long Minnesotan involved with both art and Norwegian Americans. I also checked exhibition catalogues for artists with Norwegian names that appeared frequently and/or won prizes. Few discoveries made this way got in the final group, but a list of some that probably should have is given below. Two of those included were brought to my attention late, Charles Thoresen by a distant relative who was seeking further information on him, and Andreas Larsen by a librarian at the Minneapolis Public Library who knew of him through a col-

lection of his work there. The chance and subjectivity that entered into the selection should be kept in mind when considering the statistics given in the body of the text.

There were several reasons for excluding some artists who probably rated inclusion: not enough works came to light, space and funds for getting works in the exhibition relating to this study were limited, time did not allow adequate investigation of the artists' origin. This last concern may not have been fully justified. Only one of the 27 originally chosen proved on investigation not to have Norwegian background. Only two were less than one hundred percent Norwegian, John Anderson, who had a German mother, and Charles Beck, whose father was half Swedish. Almost fifty percent were born in America, which means that the Norwegian immigrants appear at least to have married primarily within their own group regardless of what their other affiliations might have been. The precise ethnic origin of Peter Lund could not be documented although he has been considered Norwegian. He, as well as Anderson and Beck, was retained.

Painters with records that indicate they could or should have been in our group include James Anderson (early), Elmer F. Anderson, Magnus Bakke, Olaf A. Berge, Olive Boe, Erik Austen Erickson, Arthur Hanson, John Huseby, J. Theodore Johnson, Arthur Monrad Johnson, Rae McFadden Keppen, Clifford Mohn, Sigvard M. Mohn, Robert Clark Nelson, Carl Olson, Paul Olson, Andreas Peterson, Roland Rustad, and Sverre Sievertz. Artists not included because of just entering the scene around our cut-off date of 1970 were Francis Christian, William Dietrickson, William Ellingson, and Phillip Thompson.

Two categories of work not included are altarpiece painting, because it was seldom original, and completely naive painting. Margit Mindrim might be considered a hobby artist but her approach is far from naive.

Painting by Minnesotans of Norwegian Background 1870–1970 [1]

A staff member at the Minnesota Historical Society said when he heard I was doing an exhibition *Painting by Minnesotans of Norwegian Background*, "Have you found any?" Although he said it facetiously, his remark was revealing. Minnesota painters of Norwegian background do not have a strong presence in the art of the state. Of possible explanations, two stand out: lack of a central symbolic figure and of an organization.

Norwegians got their position in Minnesota politics early through the powerful senator (and previously governor) Knute Nelson (1843–1924) and have retained it through people like Walter Mondale. Their place in Minnesota literature was established by Ole Rølvaag (1876–1931) with his *Giants in the Earth* of 1927 and in music at about the same time by F. Melius Christiansen (1871–1955) and the St. Olaf Choir. There has not been a comparable figure in painting. Syd Fossum (1909–1978) could have qualified in his time but he never presented himself as Norwegian nor did the immigrant community make any effort to claim him (Ill. 39). His prominence was also short-lived.

Being without a star, the Norwegian artists of the state might have received attention through an organization, but they had none. This made their situation quite different from that of Norwegian-American artists in Chicago and Brooklyn. While the Chicago Norske Klub (Norwegian Club) was not an organization of artists, it served as a support organization for them and through the 1920s and occasionally later sponsored juried exhibitions of their work. The Norwegian Cafe of Chicago functioned in somewhat the same way, also hosting several juried shows. The judges for all these exhibitions were from outside the immigrant community, often from the Art Institute, and the openings got media coverage.

The artists themselves in the New York area organized as the Norwegian Art and Craft Club of Brooklyn in 1939. It sponsored classes and other activities as well as many exhibitions, some of which were held in non-ethnic institutions such as the Brooklyn Library and the Riverside Museum. This gave the artists exposure well outside the immigrant community. The last was held at the south branch of the Brooklyn Library in November and December of 1955. [2]

The attempts at Norwegian or even Scandinavian art organizations in Minnesota were short-lived. The earliest was the Norwegian Art Society organized by A.C. Haugan, Kristofer Janson, Nils Michelet, Andreas Ueland, Sven Oftedal, John E. Ofstie, and a Dr. Thama in March, 1887, to get Norwegian art properly represented at the Second Minneapolis Industrial Exposition later that year. They assembled a formidable loan exhibition which included at least two local immigrant artists, Haakon Melvold (1841–1888), with the only major showing he ever had (he died the following year), and Peter F. Lund (dates unknown), who had gotten in without organizational backing the previous year (Ills. 4–5,1–2). The Society was still contributing to the Exposition in 1893 when Herbjorn Gausta (1854–1924) was included as well as Melvold, now with works that the Society owned. [3] It seems to have dissolved about this time, probably because two of its members, the author and Unitarian minister Kristofer Janson and the clothier and artist John E. Ofstie, returned to Norway. It was the only strictly Norwegian art organization ever known to have existed in Minnesota, and it included only one artist, John Ofstie, who was also a businessman.

A Scandinavian Art Society of America was organized with much flair in 1914 with both Governor Eberhart and University President Vincent participating. It was openly a fund-raising effort initiated by the Minneapolis Society of Fine Arts, which then had its building under construction. The purpose was to get support for a separate area to house Scandinavian art at the Institute and funds for acquisitions to fill it. The hype of its founding dissipated, as did the society itself in the early 20s. Again a return to Norway may have entered in. Its president, Lauritz S. Svendson, resumed his position as U.S. Ambassador in Oslo in 1922. The purchase of a painting by Gustav Adolf Fjaestad and one by Helmer Mas-Olle, both Swedish, for the Institute seems to have been its major accomplishment.[4]

Of interest to us is the fact that the Society and the Institute at the time apparently had immigrant art as well as art from Scandinavia in mind. According to two reports, it was an exhibition of the Norwegian immigrant artist Lars Haukaness (1869–1929) of Chicago at the Radisson Hotel late in 1913 that got the idea of a Scandinavian art society going. The Institute itself makes clear in its May, 1914, *Bulletin* that "the term 'Scandinavian artist' is meant to include all artists of Scandinavian birth or descent." Robert Koehler (1850–1917), who was in his last year as director of the Institute, may have had something to do with this. He had been a schoolmate of the Norwegian-American Herbjorn Gausta in Munich and utilized him on the jury of the Minneapolis Art League Exhibition, 1897 (Ills. 6–10,42). The two exhibited together constantly from then until Koehler's death in 1917. Just two years earlier, his entry at the First Exhibition of Works by Minneapolis Artists was a rather formidable portrait of Gausta, now at Luther College, Decorah, Iowa.

Koehler also seems to have had a close relationship to the Norwegian-American Alex Grinager (1865–1949) who, with Koehler and Gausta, retained his membership in the small exclusive Minneapolis Art League in spite of his having left for New York in 1896. It was undoubtedly artists of this type Koehler had in mind when including immigrants among the Scandinavians to whom the special space would be dedicated. With the passing of Koehler, who was himself a German American from Milwaukee, everything changed and neither Scandinavian nor Scandinavian-American artists have since found much place at the Institute of Arts.

A Minnesota organization of Scandinavian business and professional men, the Odin Club, organized in 1899 and lasting until 1930, served as something of a support group for Scandinavian immigrant artists. In 1910 it sponsored an exhibition of twelve paintings by the just-mentioned Albert Lea artist of Norwegian background, Alex Grinager, who by then was making a name for himself in New York (Ills. 36,44).[5] It may also have had something to do with the Haukaness exhibition three years later since it intended to purchase a painting from it for the Minneapolis Society of Fine Arts. It was definitely supportive of the Scandinavian Art Society, which was founded in the Club's quarters.

The Odin Club's major venture into the arts was its Exhibition of Works by Scandinavian Artists, April 26–May 5, 1924, which was a juried exhibition of Minnesota artists with Scandinavian background. According to an article in the *Minneapolis Tribune*, April 20, it was modeled on the Norwegian and Swedish serial exhibitions in Chicago, from whose sponsors small loan exhibitions were invited. August Klagstad (1866–1949) (Ill. 50) and Herbjorn Gausta, now considered grand old men on the local Scandinavian art scene, were also given small loan exhibitions. Klagstad, however, was also on the jury and in the competitive exhibition. This turned out to be the last showing of Gausta in his lifetime. He died less than three weeks after it closed. Though it had been announced as the first in a series, nothing comparable happened again. The Club was within six years of its demise, and there may have been some dissatisfaction with the initial venture. For whatever reason the great Swedish artists of the area Knute Heldner (1877–1952) and David Ericson (1869–1946), who spent much of their time out of state, did not exhibit, nor did the precocious young Swede Dewey Albinson (1898–1971). This meant that most, if not all, awards went to Norwegians. Sverre Sieverts, Andreas Petersen, and Sigvard Mohn, who received first, second, and honorable mention awards in painting, are definitely Norwegian as is Arthur Monrad Johnson, who won the first and only award in drawing. The national background of Frederick Frederickson and Eugene Gilboe, who also received honorable mentions in painting, is not known.[6]

Ironically, the only truly national competitive exhibition for Americans of Norwegian background took place in St. Paul, the Norse-American Centennial Art Exhibition held at the State Fairgrounds June 6–9, 1925. It was part of the nationally sponsored centennial celebration of the arrival of the first immigrant ship from Norway. Of the 55 artists whose works were admitted, 21 were local. Eight of the 21 are included in this study. Two local artists won second place awards, Peter Teigen (1895–1936) in painting and Andreas R. Larsen (1877–1942) in drawing (Ills. 47,40). The two highest awards and the third in painting went to artists from the east coast. Chicagoans received only two honorable mentions.[7] The twenty local exhibitors would have made a fine core for an organization, but none developed.

Minnesota painters of Norwegian background appear to have felt that it was better to integrate than to organize. They are very much a part of the total fabric of Minnesota painting, found at all levels except the very highest from almost the beginning to the present. Both Gausta and Grinager, we recall, were early participants in the exclusive eight-member Minneapolis Art League organized in 1893, supposedly at the instigation of Koehler, as the first organization of professional artists in the area.[8] By 1897 its membership had grown to fourteen, including in addition to the two Norwegians most of the prominent artists in the city, among whom were Burt Harwood, who in 1894 was appointed director of the St. Paul School of Fine Arts; Robert Koehler, who held the comparable position in Minneapolis; and Alexis Fournier (1865–1948), the Minnesota artist who was getting the most national attention at the time.[9] Both Gausta and Grinager stayed with the organization through several transitions in title well into the twentieth century.

A second Minnesota organization of professional artists, the Attic Club organized in 1910, also had a founding member and ongoing participant of Norwegian background, Andreas R. Larsen. The group consisted largely of commercial artists (Larsen was a stained glass designer and producer) who had a desire to develop their fine arts skills as a group. Its founder was Theodore J. Keane, Koehler's assistant, from San Francisco. The submission of original work to be approved by a committee was required for membership. Larsen was on committees and assisted with projects until the organization dwindled toward the Depression and apparently died about that time. He was the only person with an identifiable Scandinavian name at the beginning, but many, primarily Norwegians, were admitted later. These included Arnold Klagstad (1898–1954) and Magnus Norstad; the latter, who lived in St. Paul, appears to have been responsible for the organization's dropping its requirement of Minneapolis residency.[10]

Minnesota painters of Norwegian background were also involved in the art organizations of the 1930s and 1940s for which art advocacy and the improvement of economic conditions for artists were major issues. The Norwegian–American Syd Fossum was the leading force in these, being a founder of The Artists' Union around 1937, which several years later became affiliated with the national organization United American Artists. The war with its better economy and emphasis on patriotism seems to have brought an end to this socialistically oriented organization. Its exhibition lists indicated that other artists of Norwegian background, including Olaf Aalbu, Jr. (b. 1917), Einar Dahl (1884–1996), and Arnold Klagstad (1898–1954) of those in this study, were also active (Ills. 37,27,51,33). On returning from service in the U.S. Army during World War II, Fossum turned his energy to Artists Equity and a more conservative group, the Minnesota Artists Association, organized about the same time as the Union. The Association lasted at least into the 1970s as a final stronghold for the Minnesota art tradition developed in the 1930s and 1940s against the onslaught of new directions from the East. Einar Dahl served a term on the board, as he did on the board of the Walker Art Center in the days of its formation around 1940. Arnold Klagstad was along in founding the Association and chaired its finance committee in 1942. But Syd Fossum was the man at the core, being made vice president in the 1940s and later president, a position he retained through the 1960s.[11]

The participation of Minnesotans with Norwegian background in non-ethnic annual exhibitions was extremely great. A recent Minnesota Historical Society study by Kay Spangler of such exhibitions in Minnesota and the artists involved between 1900 and 1970 gives the basis for some figures.[12] The number of Johnsons alone is 108, which exceeds by eight the total number of Bakers, Joneses, Millers, and Smiths combined. When the Johnsons are put together with the Andersons, Nelsons, and Olsons, the number is 287, almost three times the number with the most popular Anglican names. The percent of these that are Norwegian may be slightly less than fifty, but even this figure would well exceed that of the supposedly Anglicans. These statistics are far from scientific, but they confirm the strength of the Norwegian element in Minnesota art in spite of its low visibility.

History

After a rather slow start, painting by Minnesotans of Norwegian background falls into two major phases, the first ending in the late teens and the next beginning in the early thirties. This leaves something of a hiatus in the twenties, but that is strangely enough when two of the most important exhibitions occurred, the Scandinavian exhibition sponsored by the Odin Club of Minneapolis in 1924 and the Norwegian art exhibition organized in connection with the Norse-American Centennial of 1925 in St. Paul.

There was not an early Norwegian artist scout in Minnesota catching Indian life, the wilderness, or the beginning of settlement as did many artists of other backgrounds. This may not have had special appeal to Norwegians who could still find much of the primitive and rugged in their own country. As far as Scandinavians were concerned, it was artists from the more civilized Denmark who were drawn to the Minnesota frontier, Ferdinand Reichard (1819–1895), who gave the state its most exquisitely rendered view of St. Anthony Falls in 1857, and Peter Gui Clauson (1830–1924), who on settling here in 1869 gave us several rougher renditions of the same subject.[13] These works are now in the Minnesota Historical Society and the Minneapolis Public Library. Clauson remained but did primarily decorative work. He also offered perhaps the first professional art instruction in the state.[14] Alex Grinager took advantage of this before he went to Copenhagen in 1885 and entered the Academy of Art where his teacher had trained.

If Peter F. Lund was indeed Norwegian as he has been considered (he too could have been Danish, see "Stories of the Artists"), he was the first painter of Norwegian background active in Minnesota and his *Stormy Night* exhibited at the First Public Loan Exhibition of the Minneapolis Society of Fine Arts the year of its founding in 1883 was the first Norwegian-American painting shown publicly in the state. According to the City Directory, the year of the exhibition was Lund's first in Minneapolis, but he already had a studio in the Domestic Block and a residence at 1305 South 23rd Avenue. He must have arrived ready to establish himself as a professional artist. His position from the beginning seems to have been one of integration and it remained so through his fourteen-year residency in Minnesota. The only indication of his being Norwegian is that the Norwegian Art Society included him in their exhibit at the 1887 Exposition. He did not, judging from titles, exhibit one work with a Norwegian subject.

There is some continuity from Lund to Haakon Melvold, the second known artist of Norwegian background to settle in the state. He arrived late in 1884, perhaps little over a year after Lund, and took a studio in the Syndicate Building, where Lund had been the previous year. One must wonder if Lund, who was constantly on the move, may not have made the space available to Melvold. In 1887, both artists, as we have seen, were shown by the Norwegian Art Society at the Second Annual Minneapolis Industrial Exposition.[15]

By 1885 the twenty year old Charles Thoresen (1865–1910) too is in the picture (Ill. 11). He must have come trained and ready to test himself as an exhibiting artist because his work appears already in the Exposition of 1886, in which Lund also exhibited. Both artists participated again in the Exposition of 1888, when Melvold is shown posthumously. The next year he was in Paris, and after his return appears to have devoted his energies completely to decorating. As far as is known, he was the third professional artist from Norway in Minnesota. Gausta, who immigrated as a boy but returned to Europe for training, also links into this continuity by establishing himself in downtown Minneapolis in 1888, the year Melvold died and five years before Lund made his final shift of residence to Duluth, where he had already maintained a studio for several years. Gausta remained an ever-present although not especially visible figure on the Minneapolis art scene until his death in 1924.

During the late 80s, when Lund, Melvold, and Thoresen were exhibiting in Minneapolis, Grinager, who was the same age as Thoresen, was studying in Copenhagen. Except for a short stay in Europe in 1892–93, he lived and worked in this city from 1890 through 1896. His contact with other local artists of Scandinavian background is charmingly revealed in his story of Gausta and the distinguished Swedish sculptor Knut Okerberg (Åkerberg in Swedish) coming down to watch him paint *Boys Bathing* on the river flat (Ill. 44). Had Grinager remained in Minneapolis and made this rather than New York the site of his considerable accomplishments, he would not only have been a major link between this early phase of activity among local artists of Norwegian background and the post-1920s phase but could have been that star that would have given greater visibility to the group.

The interim period of the late teens to early thirties was not without activity. Two of our artists were ending comparatively

short careers near the beginning of it. Carl L. Boeckmann (1867–1923) who did ambitious battle scenes in the mid-teens continued to paint until his death (Ills. 3,38,43). Olaf Aalbu, Sr. (1879–1926), was still at the height of his artistic development (Ills. 24,48). Andreas Larsen entered the Twin Cities art scene in the early teens. His major period of exhibiting was the teens and twenties, and during the latter he founded his own very successful stained glass designing and production firm. In 1915 August Klagstad moved his portrait and altar painting business to Minneapolis from Marinette, Wisconsin, and entered fine art canvases of many types in the local exhibitions into the early thirties (Ill. 50). Peter Teigen (1895–1939) and Magnus Norstad (1884–1962) were active but, like Grinager, in the East. Matt Wolden, about whom little is known, was painting in Duluth but during the twenties entered only the Norwegian Club exhibitions in Chicago and the two ethnic exhibitions in the Twin Cities (Ill. 23). The new generation was also by the mid-twenties beginning to test the turf.

Sixteen of the 28 artists in this study had their most active period after the early 1930s. World War II marks a divide, but there is no sharp break, and there was at least one artist bridging it, Elmar Berge (1893–1956), whose style did not change (Ill. 49). The federal art programs from the mid-thirties through the early forties put its mark on the first half. Emphasis was on the American scene, both rural and industrial. Since it was a program of government support for the arts in a time of extreme financial need at the lower levels of the economic scale, socialistic elements entered in but were kept in check since the programs were dependent on some bipartisan support.[16]

At least five artists in our group, possibly more, were on the payroll of these federal programs at some point: Einar Dahl, Syd Fossum, Sverre Hanssen (1891–1968), Arnold Klagstad (son of August), and Axel E. Schar (1888–1984) (Ills. 32,20,). Others who worked close to its spirit and general stylistic character were Lloyd Herfindahl (1922–1996), in everything but his most satiric and surrealistic work (Ills. 21–22); Olaf

Aalbu, Jr., in his early period; Carl Olderen (1879–1959), in spite of his emphasis on form (Ills. 26,35); J. Theodore Sohner (1906–1962), except in some of the very late symbolic work; and Orabel Thortvedt (1896–1983), except in some works that are more personal than broadly historic (Ills. 12–15).

One might ask what the spirit behind and the characteristics of the art of the federal programs were, beyond what has been said. An overriding concern in all the programs was to bring art from its ivory tower back to the people, to make the artist responsible to society. Things representative of the local environment and the simple sentiments of everyday life came to dominate in subject matter and realism, generally stripped of detail, to characterize style.[17] To what extent the art of the kind referred to was determined by federal art programs and to what extent it was a direct outgrowth of something that artists like Grant Wood had established already in the 1920s is difficult to say. What is clear, however, is that a commonality exists in much art from the 1930s, including that of artists with Norwegian background. Some of that commonality is also found in the work of Margit Mindrum (1899–1975) although she was outside the art establishment and not active until the 1950s (Ills. 16–19).

All the artists mentioned who were not in the federal programs must have been eligible from a standpoint of need. I asked Olderen's son why his father didn't sign up, and he said he didn't know but he was aware that certain women in the family were strongly opposed to accepting relief. In spite of Norway's highly developed social programs today, there was a strong feeling in the old peasant culture that one did not accept relief unless circumstances, physical or mental, had so-to-speak placed one outside society as that was conceived at the time. The federal art programs were not direct relief, since the artists worked for what they got, but they could smack of that as government efforts to give financial support to segments of the society not able to earn what they needed from the private sector.

Elmar Berge was at the height of his production during the thirties and forties but falls outside the mainstream of art at the time and did not as far as is known participate in the federal programs. His landscapes and seascapes have a generic quality even when identified by title with a specific place. His style continued the loose brushstrokes of late Naturalism but with a tendency toward the sweet or sensational in coloration. The florals are a different matter, often having a wonderful freshness and strength (Ill. 49). Other than for them, much of his work belongs more in the category of popular than fine art.

A core element in what I am considering the second strain in the second phase of Norwegian-American art in Minnesota grows definitely out of the thirties but has a new twist. Cyrus Running (1913–1976), John Maakestad (b. 1928), and Charles Beck (b. 1923) all have their B.A.'s from Minnesota Lutheran colleges and M.F.A.'s from the University of Iowa (Ills. 34,28,29). They are the only artists of the 28 in this study who can be easily grouped. Running originally, and the other two through their entire careers, concentrated on local rural and small town subjects, but, more than the artists of the thirties, they penetrated beyond its surface to explore the formal and spiritual qualities in it. For Maakestad, getting at the forces behind nature as revealed in the local landscape was the major concern while Beck, as stated in his "Story" later, was exploring the expressive elements in its forms. Running's growing concern with man, theology, and architecture carried him ultimately into new directions, but he remained clearly on the same foundation as the younger men. If one were to speak of a tradition in the painting of Minnesotans with Norwegian background, it would have to be in the work of these three artists and many followers and students. Here may be the nearest thing to a Minnesota art tradition in general.

John Anderson (1923–1971) stands alone among our artists. His *Christmas* (Ill. 41) is one of his most beautiful and easily read paintings, with the complexity that sets his work apart more subtly present than usual. In the story of his life I refer to him as the artist in our group that comes nearest revealing genius, and genius cannot be classified. Anderson communicates first and foremost through pure artistic means, setting up dialogues between texture and smoothness, the painterly and unbroken colors, mass and space, the finite and the infinite, language and the visual image, or between all of these at once. He is a fine example of Peter Teigen's concept of art as idea apart from subject matter (see Tiegen's "Story"). In accordance with Teigen as well, Anderson often introduces a suggestion of objects to ensure that the idea is real. For him, however, objects may also be there to stimulate fantasy, another element of great importance in his work. The Norwegians of Minnesota could not have done better, even if they can claim only half the credit since his mother was German.

Is it coincidence that these four artists who are the latest in our group and who to me also represent the highest level of development all had arenas outside the Twin Cities? Running, Maakestad, and Beck had theirs for most of their lives in Moorhead, Northfield, and Fergus Falls, respectively. Anderson originally had his in Minneapolis, Paris, and New York, but spent his last productive eleven years in "Beck country" at Battle Lake, actually dying in Beck's home town of Fergus Falls, June 3, 1971, at only 47 years of age.

Who Were the Artists as a Group?

As stated in the Preface, the 28 artists presented in some depth in this study were selected partly by chance and without rigidly established criteria. That must be kept in mind in considering the statistics presented here. Only two proved not to be 100% Norwegian. Anderson was half German and Beck one quarter Swedish.

If we consider Peter Lund of Norwegian birth in spite of its not having been documented, fifteen of our 28 artists were born in Norway; and of these, eight had some training or involvement with art in that country. Seven came from what is now Oslo or a wide area around it with Moss to the south, Modum to the west, and Hamar to the north. Three came from north Norway, and one each from Trøndelag (the area surrounding Trondheim), Telemark, Gudbrandsdalen, and the west coast. When American-born artists are added on the basis of ancestral origins (information on the female side was not always available), the proportional distribution remains much the same: twelve from the Oslo area, four from North Norway, four from Trøndelag, three each from the west coast and Telemark, and one from Gudbrandsdalen. Lund is omitted from these figures.

The fine arts appear rather late in Norwegian immigration history, which is generally considered to have begun in 1825, so it is not surprising to find that the areas in which most of the artists have their backgrounds—around Oslo and Trondheim—are those from which mass emigration too was late.[18] The areas in which emigration occurred early and which therefore are most commonly associated with it—Stavanger, Hallingdal, Valdres, and Sogn—are scarcely represented.[19] Telemark, which also belongs in this group, is represented but with a special type of artist that will be commented on later.

The early immigrants were largely farmers who continued as farmers, struggling with wresting a living from the prairie. They had neither the time nor the circumstances for cultivating the fine arts. But there may be another reason for the fine arts being more prevalent among this later group of immigrants.

In the areas around Trondheim and Oslo, where the land was comparatively flat and the farms comparatively large, the rural culture was becoming increasingly urbanized by the mid-nineteenth century. Pictures on the walls, for example, were not unusual here while in the inner valleys of Telemark, Hallingdal, Valdres, and even much of Gudbrandsdal, art followed the early folk tradition of being limited to furniture and other functional objects or to the walls themselves. The more favorable economic circumstances in the areas from which most of our artists came accounted in part for the later emigration, but the more urbanized culture in them would also have made the people leaving them more prepared for cultivating the fine arts than were those from the inner valleys and west coast. It may be significant that two of the three artists with Telemark background are the women Margit Mindrum and Orabel Thortvedt, who continued to work in something of a folk tradition in spite of painting pictures for the wall. With the exception of Orabel's jaunt into doing pets for the wealthy, both operated within the framework of a local rural community.

In spite of there being some rationale for the way the statistics turned out, the comparatively strong representation from North Norway seems to call for further explanation. For the artists from there who were trained or oriented toward art before leaving—Aalbu, Sr., Hanssen, and Olderen—it may have been the limited possibilities for artists in this somewhat remote area and concern for the competition in Oslo or Bergen that led to their choosing Minneapolis, a metropolitan area that was still not too threatening and where competition was probably less than in southern Norway. The total absence of the inner valleys—Valdres, Hallingdal, Østerdalen—and the weak representation from the west coast seems strange and may be due to chance.

The demographics of American-born artists has no real surprises. Three were born in the Twin Cities, six in outlying areas of Minnesota, and four in surrounding states. Two of the latter, Running and Maakestad, were the sons of pastors who were constantly on the move; one, Arnold Klagstad, was the son of an artist who came for greater patronage than was to be found in Marinette, Wisconsin; and the last, Syd Fossum, came from South Dakota to go to art school. None came from farther than adjoining states, which indicates that Minnesota was not an art mecca for more than the region immediately surrounding it.

The strength of outlying Minnesota, of course, reflects the large rural element in the Norwegian population of the state. When we look at where our artists established themselves, the figures are reversed. Of the entire 28, seventeen were settled in the Twin Cities and only eight in outlying areas. Three who got their start in the state—Grinager, Teigen, and Norstad—settled in the East.

Considering the precariousness of art as a profession, it is surprising to learn that eight of our 28 painters made their living from the fine arts and fourteen from them together with related work such as decorating, designing, restoration, and the like. The decorators, to be sure, in slack periods had to fill in with house painting. Only five got or supplemented their income with work outside the plastic arts: Sohner with singing, Schar with photography and journalism, Dahl with making artificial limbs, and the two women Thortvedt and Mindrum with work on their farms. Mindrum alone could be considered an amateur, but even she for a period operated much as a professional with many commissions.

Much has been made of the close relationship between art and literature in late nineteenth century Norway. There is some indication of that in Norwegian Minnesota as well. A good part of Thortvedt's history painting and drawing is related to a historic novel on which she was working; Schar functioned as both an artist and a journalist; Dahl wrote "outsider" spiritualist poetry; and Hanssen enlightened his daughter in a letter by quoting a poem which ends, "From servitude to freedom's home, Free thou thy mind in bondage bent."

But music is the sister art closest to our painters. Olaf Aalbu, Sr., came trained in both it and art, questioning for a time which one to pursue. Sohner never could decide, and his career may have suffered from that. Dahl was on his way to drum for an Indian powwow when he saw the view near Mazeppa that led to *Mystic Hollow*. Cyrus Running was famous for his Victor Borge style act, I Hate Music. Herbjorn Gausta told Carl Hansen of the response aroused in him by just the tune-up notes on the Norwegian folk instrument, the Hardanger fiddle. John Anderson included in his response to the proverbial question about favorite artists on a form from the Walker Art Center, Bach, Beethoven, Mozart, Billie Holiday, and Satchmo. Music comes up somewhere in the material on almost every artist. The cultural circle that brought artists and writers together in Norway did not exist here, but music in some form was ever present.

There were few if any "professional Norwegians" among the artists. The senior Klagstad was a founder of the Modum-Eiker Lag for people from his province, but he was also a dedicated Mason. Boeckmann donated a painting for resale to support the Kristiania Lag, but he dressed, according to his obituary, to look "as if he just stepped out of the Latin Quarter." Similarly Herfindahl talked in his late years of founding a Norse society but generally made more of his connection with Monaco and the Left Bank in Paris than with Norway. Though Teigen's father was one of the founders of the Sons of Norway, I came across only two references to artists in our group being members. Even the Lutheran Church is not overwhelmingly present except in the lives of the altar painters Gausta and the elder Klagstad and the artists affiliated with Lutheran colleges. Hanssen was a professed agnostic. Christian Science literature was found in Teigen's papers. Schar was buried from a Methodist church, and a great number of the artists were buried from funeral homes without reference to clergy.

As mentioned at the beginning, the painters of Norwegian background in Minnesota didn't represent a uniform, closely knit group. There is even little information about informal communication among them. The story of Gausta watching Grinager paint *Boys Bathing* is a touching exception, but there is no indication of ongoing contact even between these two. The Olderens knew Einar Dahl, but the relationship, according to their son, was dependent on circumstance. Aalbu, Jr., admired Fossum but contact between the two was limited. Apparently the closest relationship existed between Herfindahl and Elmar Berge. This is mentioned by acquaintances of Herfindahl and documented by a drawing he made of Berge, one of his best. On the whole, the artists seem to have maintained an isolationist position in relation to each other and preferred being absorbed into the larger art scene.

Patronage

Patronage is a subject on which it is very difficult to get precise information, but it may have contributed to the low profile assumed by the artists as Norwegians. Patronage for local art in general in Minnesota has been a problem. The area has an inferiority complex about itself. The Scandinavian immigrant, as we now know through Garrison Keillor, is looked on as the epitome of that uppermidwesterness about which we feel inferior. Why, then, flaunt something that might backfire on the local market.

A wonderful story, probably exaggerated, that represents the problem of the Scandinavians on the local art scene is said to have appeared in a newspaper at the time Martin Friedman, director of the Walker Art Center, was negotiating with pop artist Claes Oldenburg (b. 1929) for the *piece de resistance* in his sculpture garden. The then established master was apparently given carte blanche as to subject matter and came with a design based on a Viking ship. Friedman reportedly pounded the table and said, "We are not going to have a Viking ship in our sculpture garden." Oldenburg, of Swedish background himself and not having experienced the local cultural climate, saw no problem in symbolizing Minneapolis as others saw it, a city of Scandinavian immigrants, but this hit a sore spot in the local art establishment. The immigrant artists in more subtle ways probably got the message that Oldenburg did, don't stress being Scandinavian if you want commissions in Minnesota. He came back with a cherry on a spoon, and everything was fine.

The local artist who presented himself as Norwegian was in a catch-22 situation. He didn't carry the image that the fine arts patrons of the state were looking for, and his own people, who should have had no problem with the image, simply were not very good patrons of art. Gausta got some early patronage, largely portraits, from the church-related elite, the Koren, Preus, and Estrem families. Mrs. Theodore Mohn of St. Olaf College raised the fifty dollars necessary for the purchase of Gausta's *The Secret* (Ill. 42) for the parlor of the "Ladies Hall" at the College, its first art acquisition, but patronage from this group seems to have been personal and did not carry over to later periods or other immigrant artists.

Starving Melvold in the 1880s did not as far as is known sell one painting to families of the type mentioned above. His presence was announced to the immigrant community through a long and laudatory article in the Minneapolis Norwegian paper *Budstikken*, February 24, 1885, shortly after his arrival. It speaks of wealthy patrons, but his obituary in the *Minneapolis Tribune*, July 24, 1888, indicates that these had been few. It mentions leaving "a wife and small children in straitened circumstances." His only known sales were to Geo. A. Bracket, apparently not Norwegian; Andreas Ueland, already a judge; Lars Rand; and A. C. Haugen, a member of the Norwegian Art Society that also appears to have bought some works for later exhibition, possibly posthumously.[20] One wonders why P. F. Lund during the same period was, judging from his life style, flying high. It may have been that he does not appear to have presented himself as Norwegian, if indeed he was, nor in any way catered to the Norwegian group. Not one of his many somewhat generic marine paintings, we recall, mentions Norway in the title, and coverage of Lund in a Norwegian newspaper has as yet not been found. He had, of course, the advantage of a dramatic style that made immediate impact, while Melvold was a meticulous academic realist.

During the century covered by this study, Norwegian-American artists in Minnesota never had one major patron or collector that has surfaced. Having one could have meant more than just the support of that person. There is a competitive element in collecting. If something is bought by one person, others also become interested. A friend of mine once made the remark, which sounds as if it could have come from Alexander Pope, "The greatest joy of collecting is to make your friends jealous." The competitive situation in which this psychology can operate did not develop for local

Norwegian-American artists. That, in itself, has contributed to their lack of visibility. In Chicago the Norwegians had at least the institutions that sponsored the ethnic exhibitions as patrons. The Norwegian Club built up a collection of fifty or more major works which were exhibited on their walls the year around, drawing attention to the very artists who in the 1920s and later would appear in the annual sales exhibitions. The owners of Norwegian hospitals, rest homes, etc. also became patrons. Nothing comparable happened here. There was not, to be sure, the convenient market that the ethnic exhibitions in Chicago offered, but the Scandinavian paintings were available here as well, only integrated with the American in non-ethnic exhibitions. The artists did exhibit, as evidenced by the 108 Johnsons, the 73 Andersons, and 64 Olsons that showed their work in Minnesota serial exhibitions between 1900 and 1970.[21] They must have had buyers but not as a group or necessarily as Scandinavians.

Only one of the artists of those presented here, Elmar Berge, is known to have had at least one major private patron. Her name was Marge Dockerty, for whom the ethnic does not seem to have been the major attraction. Scenes of Norwegian type or title had no special prominence in her collection of about 65 Berges that were sold at auction in her home town of Rochester in 1998.

What Did the Artists Paint

Except for a small body of works that depict Norway and the sea, mostly at the beginning of our period, Minnesota artists of Norwegian background painted primarily what other artists in the area were painting: rural life and landscape, the city, hard times, works of celebration (including sacred subjects), people as people (portraits and genre), and art as art (still lifes and abstractions). If there is one characteristic that sets them somewhat apart it is a tendency toward regionalism, not that specific category of American art represented by Grant Wood but painting of the immediate surroundings and the activities belonging to them. Only Herfindahl, and occasionally Dahl and Running, can get philosophical.

Exotic subjects or things observed in travel outside the region are rare. History painting is found only in Thortvedt, whose subjects are Minnesotan and from a recent past with which she was well familiar. She even knew her hero, Ola Thortveidt, who died when she was about seven (Ill. 13). She paints him as she would have seen him from a slightly low angle and as a real grandpa with beard. In spite of his patriarchal dignity, one has the feeling he is ready to accept her in his lap. Much of the work with which we are concerned has this kind of immediacy, intimacy, and air of the real that makes regionalism seem like the appropriate term. It is very Minnesotan.

Norway and the Sea

Norway and the sea play a far smaller role in the painting of Minnesotans with Norwegian background of this period than is generally assumed. These subjects belong largely to the early decades and almost exclusively to painters of Norwegian birth and training who had difficulty adjusting to new subject matter. Melvold is the classic example (Ills. 4–5). The tradition in which he was brought up stems from Dusseldorf, Germany, where his teacher trained. It involved the careful study of nature but with its details put together in studio compositions. These tended to run rather to stereotypes and had been arrived at for the Norwegian landscape by Norway's many Dusseldorf-trained artists and Johan Christian Dahl (1788–1857), who worked in Dresden before them. In the total of five years Melvold was in America, four in Minneapolis, he must have continued to make studies from nature. It could not otherwise be depicted so exquisitely in his work, but not one of Melvold's completed paintings has a title that indicates the subject is American. One suspects that he looked considerably at Minnehaha Falls when working on his large falls painting (Ill. 5), but if this is indeed the falls he exhibited at the Minneapolis Industrial Exposition of 1887, he placed it in Gudbrandsdalen, Norway.

Gausta is the second artist thoroughly grounded in Norwegian subjects who had to adjust to the American scene. Having in the late seventies and early eighties studied in Munich where he would have been exposed to the work of such budding German Naturalists as Wilhelm Leibl (1844–1900), who created their whole compositions from the observation of nature, he was much better prepared than Melvold to portray new subject matter. His fresh and quite genuinely American *Washington Prairie Parsonage* (Ill. 9) was created only two years after he had been making sketches for paintings like *Summertime* (Ill. 8) in his native Telemark on his way back from Munich.

But the Norwegian landscape also stayed with Gausta and remained the subject of at least half his easel paintings. His memory of it was reinforced by several later trips home when he also took photographs, some of which were used as the basis for paintings. Gausta is known to have painted at least one specific view in Norway for a patron here,[22] but he did not make a business of painting the Norwegian homes of immigrants as some of the Norwegian-American artists in Chicago did. His Norwegian paintings can seem a bit repetitious, but they are not generic. They are invariably from the regions of Tinn and Rauland in Telemark (Ill. 7–8), where his parents were from, or nearby coastal areas such as Breivik (Ill. 6). He never painted the west coast fjords that are most symbolic of Norway. His generation of young Realists and Naturalists who left Oslo in the 1870s to study in Munich reacted against the earlier romantics who concentrated their efforts on the fjords. Gausta remained completely consistent to this position. There is no evidence of his ever having visited Norway's fjord country.

Peter Lund, the first Norwegian artist—if indeed Norwegian—active in Minnesota, had no great adjustment to make because the sea and ships are much the same all over the western world, and they are what he generally painted. As mentioned, he avoided specific reference to Norway either visually or in the titles of his works, but many could be considered Norwegian if one preferred. The works shown here (Ill. 1–2) have that flexibility.

The only later painter before 1970 in whose work Norwegian subjects have some prominence is Carl L. Boeckmann. These were not landscapes but portraits of Norway's great men: Ibsen, Bjornsen, Grieg, a heroic sea pilot Ulabrand, and many generic pilot heads that were apparently a good sales item. The one shown (Ill. 3) is the largest known in oil although there is a comparable watercolor. This oil is also the most freely painted of the Boeckmann pilot heads known to me, which suggests it may have been done early when Boeckmann was still under the spell of the Norwegian Naturalists with whom he professed to have had contact or it is an anomaly of the kind that can occur in Boeckmann. Much of his work is more linear and tightly painted. He, like Gausta, seems to have retained the Naturalists' rejection of the fjords although one very small fjord painting is known. Views of Lake Minnetonka, on the other hand, are common.

Other artists who occasionally painted Norwegian subjects are Elmar Berge, who made several short trips back to paint in the Stavanger area from where he came, and Sverre Hanssen, who had vivid memories of the sea from his time as a fisherman that he would occasionally put on canvas. These works, however, are incidental in their overall production (Ills. 49,32).

The situation in Minnesota as far as subjects from Norway are concerned differs totally from that in Chicago, where the dominant subject matter of the three major painters—Karl Ouren (1882–1943), Ben Blessum (1877–1954), and Emil Biorn (1864–1934)—is Norwegian. Even the generic landscapes and seascapes of the popular Chicago painters John Hammerstad (1842–1925), Svend Svendson (1864–1945), and Gulbrand Sether (1869–1941) showed scenes that were generally more suggestive of Norway than America.[23]

One can only speculate on why there should be this difference. During the period of the exhibitions in Chicago when painters knew they would be having primarily ethnic audiences, this is understandable; but that was for only ten or so years after 1920 and the difference is evident much earlier. It might be for the same reason that the ethnic exhibitions themselves came into being there. Chicago because of its size alone was overwhelming to Norwegian immigrants. Norwegianness was something they could find shelter in, something that had boundaries they could relate to. Minneapolis did not offer quite the same threat because it was smaller and Scandinavians had a much greater part in the whole. In fact, as demonstrated by the Walker sculpture garden story, it was the Americans here who were on the defensive. The artists of Norwegian background and the Norwegian-American art public in Minneapolis could be more relaxed about their ethnicity because its presence was assumed, for better or for worse, as part of the population of the city.

Just at the end of our period a demand for art with Norwegian subject matter and artists to supply it came on the scene in Minneapolis as well. In the 1970s and 1980s Frances Christian acquired a substantial clientele for her colorful impressionistic views of Norway, and at the same time the semi-blind commercial artist Floyd Johnson built up a thriving business in paintings and prints with Viking subjects. The wave apparently subsided in the late eighties when Christian considerably expanded her subject matter and Johnson began moving toward western subjects and ultimately moved west himself.

Rural Life and Landscape

Rural life and landscape runs as a consistent theme in the work of Minnesota artists with Norwegian background from Gausta's 1883 painting of the rural parsonage at Washington Prairie near Decorah, Iowa, about fifteen miles south of the Minnesota border (Ill. 9), through the works of the final threesome in our study, Running, Beck, and

Maakestad (Ill. 34, 24, 28). It is therefore possible here more than in any other category of subject matter to follow stylistic developments in the treatment of the subject.

The earliest presentations are deceptively idyllic, the rural parsonage in a sense being an extension of the city into the country. Early Norwegian-American parsonages, like this one, were in actuality also farms from which the pastor was expected to get some of his income. The artist has chosen to show it at a moment of leisure, perhaps a Sunday afternoon, when the impression is of a small manor house in Norway. It is from such an environment that both Reverend Ulrik and Mrs. Elisabeth Koren who lived here had come twenty years earlier. Both the painting of the exterior and of the comfortably furnished pastor's study (Ill. 10), which may date slightly later, were probably gifts to the Korens in appreciation of financial assistance given the young Gausta for his studies in Europe. He is known to have given such gifts to others who had helped him get established as an artist. The warm and cozy interior, not a simple task to paint, brings to mind work of the American William Merritt Chase (1849–1916), whom Gausta may have met in Munich since Gausta has written his New York address in one of his early sketchbooks.

The freshness of Gausta's Naturalism in the above two works, not quite so evident in all of his painting, is lacking in Charles Thoreson's *Landscape* (Ill. 11). It, on the other hand, reveals a superb sense for creating the illusion of masses, space, and atmosphere through subtle nuances of color. It is a masterpiece of sheer craftsmanship; and as a decorator, Thoreson probably considered it a study for a panel to be incorporated into a wall decoration. Thoreson's treatment of details in nature, as seen in his drawings (see inside covers), show the same finesse and sense for decorative qualities that are found in his landscape.

Orabel Thortvedt's brown cocker spaniel pastel (Ill. 12) has some of the same subtle manipulation of color and decorative qualities found in Thoreson's work about forty years earlier, but she was also capable of depicting the more rugged aspects of rural life. The portrait of her grandfather (Ill. 13) is being looked at here rather than in the section on people because it makes a statement about pioneer life in general as much as it does about an individual. Behind him is the wintry prairie of Houston county in the process of settlement, the place from which Ola Thortveidt led a caravan of fellow Norwegians to virgin territory on the Buffalo River east of Moorhead in the Red River Valley. He is shown with the marks of hard work and determination but also as a man who has arrived. The traditional Norwegian log chair of his own making on which he sits reveals the firmness of his self-built foundation, and the watch chain with fob reveals that he is now a man of distinction and substance.

A story of hard work and simple living is told as well in Orabel's drawing of her great great grandmother (Ill. 14), who also took the trek north after first having crossed the Atlantic ten years earlier, already a grandmother. Orabel's mastery in depicting animals—the restless horses, oxen, and dog—finds expression in the drawing of the caravan setting up camp for the night (Ill. 15).

The farm life in Houston county that Orabel's family left in 1870 has been touchingly recorded by her contemporary Margit Mindrum (Ill. 16–19). There are a number of similarities in situation and background between the artists although they may never have been aware of each other. They were both farm women who had the tenacity and drive to make art careers for themselves, each in her own way. Mindrum had the disadvantage of having to wait until she was past fifty around the year 1950 to launch her short but impressive career. She also had to solve her own technical problems since she had no formal art training. Both she and Orabel, however, had the advantage of stemming from the cultural elite peasantry of Telemark where there had long been recognition of art as a part of life.

Mindrum painted what she saw around her in a style informed more by photography and popular prints than by the fine arts. This gives her work a freshness and authenticity that can be almost uncanny. To her the activities of farm life, partly based on memory to be sure, are totally integrated with the landscape in which they occur, all being the reflection of a higher order that is very real to her. The title of her memoirs *No Change My Heart Shall Fear,* is revealing of her religious faith. In her integration of the spiritual with rural life and landscape she has an affinity with her contemporaries Running, Beck, and Maakestad though they are in approach and style miles from her.

The relation of human activity to landscape is also marvelously brought together in Axel E. Schar's *Logging Drive on River* (Ill. 20). The figures almost become one with the logs and the movement of the water. Here, however, one feels more of a physical integration of man's energies with those of nature than an all-encompassing spiritual presence.

The penetrating vision of Lloyd Herfindahl presents the other side of the man/nature coin as found in rural Minnesota. He sees the lack of place for the feminine and the presence of a certain vulgarity in rural life. His *Captive* (Ill. 21) shows the farmer's wife with a basket of apples from barren trees in a barren landscape looking over a fence which through a phantom shadow appears to imprison her. Nature has lost its color and become a monotonous yellow. In his *Threshing Time* (Ill. 22) he makes a similar statement but in another way. Sedate women in the background are serving a macho, gluttonous threshing crew that dominates the foreground. Here he shows us the essentially animal nature that can exist in people whose lives are consumed by eeking out a living from the land. The view we get of farming in these two works is diametrically opposed to the one we get in Herfindahl's *Homage to Agriculture* which in 1986 was in the Cenex Corporation Minnesota headquarters. It is to his credit that he considered both.

All the paintings so far have presented rural Minnesota quite realistically or, in the case of Herfindahl, symbolically and satirically. A number of painters tried to catch the element of transcendental beauty in it or concentrate on the expressive elements in its forms. To the former belong two artists, Matt Wolden, who through pastel colors and delicate brushwork gives an ethereal quality to his *Meadow in Bloom*

(Ill. 23) and Olaf Aalbu, Sr., who gives supernatural vibrance to *Winter River* (Ill. 24) through the dominance of white and blue, the latter intensified by its complement in the yellow tones of the exposed canvas.

For the rest of the painters in this group, the *forms* of nature have been of overriding importance. Cezanne appears to be the inspiration behind the faceting of elements in Arnold Klagstad's *Ilgen Falls* (Ill. 25) from 1940 and Olderen's more extremely geometricized *Golden Valley Farm* (Ill. 26) from ten years earlier. In it one actually finds Cezanne's proverbial cubes, cones, and spheres. Einar Dahl's *Mystic Hollow* (Ill. 27) of 1939–1941 gets its aesthetic character from the curvilinear movements in the landscape, their intersecting, and their dialogue with the geometry of buildings. The formal elements of the painting relate it to the abstractions Dahl was working on at the time, as seen in *Basic Forms* (Ill. 51), which had its origin around 1940 though the version shown here is from 1961. Although he as a semi-professional may not have been known to Maakestad and Beck, he foreshadows the expressive use of the curvilinearity of Minnesota's hills found in their work (Ill. 28, 29). The link is probably Grant Wood.

The City

It may have been the attraction of opposites that led Minnesota painters with Norwegian background to urban subject matter. The first generation of immigrant painters were largely from rural areas though many from the general vicinity of Oslo. Those born here, as the statistics showed, were also generally from the country. The earliest known indications of an urban attraction are drawings in Charles Thoreson's sketchbooks that include a well-conceived and superbly executed view of Duluth from the corner of First Street and Fifth Avenue West dated 1890 (Ill. 30). He may never have *painted* a cityscape because he was channeled early into decorative work, and bucolic themes were more appropriate in it. Around the same time, Gausta did a view of Hennepin Avenue in Minneapolis closely related to the one at the Minneapolis Institute of Arts by Robert Koehler. It is in private possession and has never been published.

The high period of city painting in Minnesota was from the late teens to World War II, and the Norwegians had a part in it. Magnus Norstad has generally been credited with painting the ultimate view of St. Paul, *The City on a Hill* (Ill. 31), which not only received both the silver medal and the highest rating in a popular ballot at a 1917 juried exhibition in the St. Paul Institute of Arts but was purchased by that institution. It has competition, however, in Sverre Hanssen's WPA production *Train Yards* (Ill. 32) from about 1940. This is less lyrical but also beautifully combines the elements of rivertown, railway center, and metropolis in its more academic way.

The painter in our group who might be called the city portraitist of Minneapolis was Arnold Klagstad, for whom the pure forms of the grain elevators in their pristine white were the major attraction (Ill. 33). It was the power plant on the St. Anthony side of the river, however, that became a dominant foreground for the elevators in the Klagstad painting bought in 1940 by the Metropolitan Museum of Art in New York as its first purchase of a work by a Minneapolis artist.[24] Klagstad appears to have gained some inspiration from Charles Sheeler (1883–1965) and other American Precisionists but, unlike them, he always retained elements of landscape as a foil for the geometry of the buildings. In this sense he also differs from the slightly later Cyrus Running who, while important in the development of what might be called the Minnesota landscape tradition represented here by Beck and Maakestad (Ills. 29,28), was largely a painter of architecture. The landscapes in which his small towns appear are generally also architecturalized and his cities are usually pure geometry, as seen in his *Urban Renewal #14* (Ill. 34).

Running's urban renewal painting is unusual as an artist's perception because it reveals no sense of loss in the process. This would have been felt by Olderen, who found the perfect subject for his faceting of forms to be the quaint little houses of squatters seen in *River Flats in Winter* (Ill. 35) of

1930. An attraction to the passing implicit in Olderen's *River Flats* was obvious in Einar Dahl's late work which was concentrated on the buildings of old Robbinsdale.

A similar kind of fascination for the city is also found among the Minnesota painters of Norwegian background who went abroad to study. It was precisely the age and picturesqueness of Europe's urban centers that appealed. An early indication of this is Grinager's *Venice* (Ill. 36) from 1894, painted only months before *Boys Bathing* (Ill. 44) and clearly in the handling of light a preparatory work for it. Half a century later Olaf Aalbu, Jr., found the same type of attraction in Paris (Ill. 37), where he studied under the GI bill.

Hard Times

Periods of difficulty, the wars and the Depression, were not avoided by the artists with whom we are concerned. Nothing specific is known about what led to Carl L. Boeckmann's oil sketch *Colonel Hans C. Heg and the 15th Wisconsin at Chickamauga, 1861* (Ill. 38) painted around 1915. There must have been talk of a commission, probably among veterans interested in having the battle memorialized, but this did not come through. Rather than stressing the heroic, Boeckmann has given us the mass murder of battle, allowing the mounted hero, Colonel Heg whose life was lost, practically to disappear among his soldiers. This could have had something to do with a commission not resulting. Syd Fossum, after serving as an artillery man in World War II exhibited two strong paintings based on his experience, *Hanau in Ruins* and *The Wehrmacht Returns*. But Fossum's major documents of hard times come from the Depression in the previous decade. What strikes us in *The Meeting* (Ill. 39) of 1937 is the crosscut section it gives of the destitute.

Celebration

To many Norwegian-Americans there was a close association between art and celebration, primarily the celebration of Christmas. This was when the largest Norwegian Lutheran publishing house, Augsburg, of Minneapolis, put out its one arts publication, *Jul i Vesterheimen* (Christmas in our western home), which later became *The Christmas Annual*. It started early in the century and lasted until 1997, reaching every part of the country where there was a Norwegian Lutheran church. It covered music and literature as well as pictorial arts, but as part of the latter included art reproductions, sometimes suitable for framing. These would occasionally be of works by Norwegian-American artists. John Maakestad recalls its impact on him as an art-starved boy. Four of Gausta's paintings reached much of Norwegian America this way. Whether or not Andreas R. Larsen was ever used in the production of the magazine I do not know, but his watercolor designs for stained glass windows, of which many have been preserved in Special Collections at the Minneapolis Public Library, have much in common with the graphics of this publication. The Larsen *Resurrection* (Ill. 40) is not typical in that it departs from the Medieval and is nearer turn-of-the-century Art Nouveau. The figures are elongated and undulating and in sensuous combinations of reds set off by blue.

In spite of John Anderson's financial and personal problems, there is something celebrative about much that he did. This is usually not specific, just a quality created by kites, carnival images, and the like in nondescript spaces. But in the tree panel of his four-part work *Christmas* (Ill. 41), there is no question of what is being celebrated. The painting is dated 1970, and if it was actually painted at Christmas that year, it would have been little more than six months before his death. Its obvious subject relates it to the return to the representational found in the late work of other abstract artists. Examples are Jackson Pollack (1912–1956) and Minnesota's own Cameron Booth (1892–1980). Some of Anderson's visual ambiguity is here, but there is more playing with flat surfaces than with depth. The idea of celebration is present not only in the tree and its accruements but in music, suggested by stylized keyboards, and in words. These, unless I am missing something, have no specific meaning, just playing around with things like the French

and English "the," but they convey a childlike abandonment, the tra-la-la, of Christmas.

People as People: Portraiture and Genre

Figure painting is not strong in the art of Norwegians in Minnesota. In this it echoes the art of Norway, but the distance is so great that direct carryover is not likely. An orientation toward nature that gave the environment precedence over man, of course, could have been transferred in family culture that had no specific reference to art. This orientation may account for Norwegian-American altar painting consisting primarily of copies. The artists did not dare take on free figural composition. Portraiture, however, did exist in immigrant art, and was among the specialties of Gausta, Boeckmann, August Klagstad, and Sohner. Since Klagstad worked largely from photographs, he is not represented here as a portraitist but as a still life painter (Ill. 50).

Much of the figure painting that does exist outside of portraiture is of a genre type such as Grinager's *Boys Bathing* (Ill. 44) or Boeckmann's delightful *Family Reading the Minneapolis Journal* (Ill. 43). The occasion for the latter may have been moving into a new house, something the Boeckmanns are known to have done in 1915, the year of the painting. The fashionable upholstered chair stands in sharp contrast to the daybed with its traditional striped Norwegian coverlet on the right. The genre element lies in such things as the torn-apart paper from which each family member has taken his or her favorite section and gone to his or her favorite spot. This is no formal family portrait. Gausta's *The Secret* (Ill. 42) is also a genre painting in that the action is as important as the figures themselves. Specific models, however, were used, Professor Gisle Bothne's daughter Anna and a cousin of the artist. Gausta's training in Munich had been in this kind of painting rather than landscape, which he turned to rather late. His *Young Mother* (Ill. 7) too reflects this background.

Sohner's official portraits can sometimes be disappointing, but his Aunt Josephine Brack (Ill. 45) and her daughter Ione (Ill. 46), both of whom were close to him, show the loving attention that can create fine painting. He was in his early twenties and still without the manners in painting that belonged to his time.

For Teigen it was not so much the person but the painting that counted, as seen in *Young Man With Kimono* (Ill. 47). He takes us from looking at people to looking at art for its own sake.

Art as Art: Still Lifes and Abstractions

All decoration is in one sense art for art's sake and Aalbu, Sr., Grinager, Hanssen, Olderen, and Thoreson devoted much of their lives to it, but the record of that is largely lost. The fact that Aalbu was primarily a decorator is clearly evident in his *Sunflowers* (Ill. 48) which is exceptional as a Minnesota painting from the twenties because of its strong design qualities and Van Gogh approach to the application of paint. It stands in sharp contrast to Elmar Berge's *Peonies* (Ill. 49) from about 25 years later, which is vigorously painted, to be sure, but still in a late Naturalist tradition. It is not even impressionistic in the strict sense because the colors are not prismatically broken down. The difference in these two works is not necessarily in quality but in approach.

August Klagstad, who in his portraits and altar paintings is the most conservative of all the later artists, in his easel paintings can be quite advanced. His boldly executed *Still Life* (Ill. 50), apparently the one he exhibited at the State Fair in 1931, is definitely under Cezanne influence. His son Arnold had spent six months studying in Paris that very year, and one must wonder if he may not have gotten home in time to have had some impact on his father before he painted his state fair entry.

Total abstraction was rare among the painters of Norwegian background in Minnesota before 1970. The kind that grew out of Cubism was rare in Minnesota painting in general. Notable exceptions are the three dimensional painted wall pieces of Charles Biederman (b. 1906) in Red Wing and the very late work of the Swede Elof Wedin (1901–1983). The abstraction that Cameron Booth

brought back from Paris and New York was more rooted in Abstract Expressionism, and even it was a passing phase in Minnesota painting. Anderson occasionally produced work without recognizable images, but there was a surrealistic element in them that set them apart from pure abstraction.

Einar Dahl's abstractions are an enigma in the art of the area (Ill. 51). They originate early, about the time he was working on *Mystic Hollow* (Ill. 27) in the late thirties. We have seen in it how he enjoyed letting one form intersect another as if both were transparent. It is this principle which he continues in a number of his abstractions but adds curious light and shade effects and the impression of planes being at odd angles. These give a poetical ambiguity to the space. Although *Basic Forms* is dated 61, it appears in a form very near this in a newspaper clipping at the Minneapolis Public Library, Special Collections, stamped April 2, 1940. It is probably the one Dahl exhibited at the Minnesota State Fair as *Abstract Composition* in 1939. During the fifties abstractions are mentioned in the notices of Dahl's exhibitions at the Rainbow Cafe, a respected venue at the time, and the American-Swedish Institute. He draws attention to the abstractions at the latter in a letter to the editor, but there is no indication of response from the public. The common people would not have understood him and those who knew art probably could not believe what they saw. His mention in that letter of concepts like our having to become the subconscious if we are "to contact the cosmic intelligence of the universe" may not have helped him. He saw his abstractions as representing a higher order of communication, and when one sees how good at least some of them are, one wonders if he might not be right.

I said at one point, and I believe much else of what I have said supports it, that a tendency toward regionalism is the predominant character in the Norwegian-American painting of Minnesota. This, as we have also seen, exists not so much as a thing apart but as an integral component in Minnesota art in general. According to the late Professor Donald Torbert, the "regionalism" in that element would make it distinctive but in a way that could be taken as perjorative. He says in *A Century of Art and Architecture in Minnesota* that "None of the better Minnesota artists have made a fetish of the local scene or subscribed to the idea that moral superiority accrued when an artist painted his own backyard." I have found no indication of fetishness and certainly not of a moral scale in subject matter among Minnesota painters of Norwegian background; but who is going to be sure? The inclination to paint what was around them that they followed naturally, it appears, puts them in a somewhat questionable position in relation to the mainstream as defined by at least some factions in the art establishment. But mainstreams are not in history itself; they are in the way we look at it. That, in a sense, is what this presentation is all about.

Notes

l. Backnoting in this essay is sparse because it is based heavily on the material in the "Stories of the Artists" for which sources are given at the end of the volume. Other sources are the exhibition catalogues, artists' files, and city directories in the Minneapolis Public Library, Special Collections (MPL-SC) and the libraries of the Minneapolis Institute of Arts (MIA) and the Minnesota Historical Society (MHS). The amount of information from these is too great and the units too small to make complete referencing feasible.

2. Rolf H. Erickson, "Norwegian-American Artists' Exhibitions Described in Checklists and Catalogs," *Norwegian-American Studies 31* (Northfield MN, 1986), 283–304. All Norwegian-American exhibitions for which there are known catalogues or checklists are referred to. This includes four Scandinavian exhibitions in Brooklyn and New York sponsored by a Society of Scandinavian Artists between 1926 and 1939. Only August Klagstad and Theodore Sohner of artists living in Minnesota participated, each just once.

3. Carl G. O. Hansen, *My Minneapolis* (Minneapolis, 1956), 92. Exposition catalogues.

4. *Bulletin of the Minneapolis Institute of Arts,* III, 3 (Mar. 19l4), 35; and 5 (May, 1914), 50. Hansen, *My Minneapolis,* 177.

5. *St. Paul Pioneer Press,* Mar. 13, 1910; typewritten copy furnished by Viva Grinager. Hansen, *My Minneapolis,* 177, 249.

6. Sybil Farmer, "Scandinavian Art Exhibit Series of Odin Club Opened," *Minneapolis Journal,* Apr. 27, 1924. Catalogue in MPL-SC.

7. Catalogue at Vesterheim.

8. Thomas O'Sullivan, "Robert Koehler and Painting in Minnesota, 1890–1915," *Art and Life on the Upper Mississippi 1890–1915* (Newark, DE, 1994), 97.

9. Catalogue of the Minneapolis Art League, Third exhibition, 1897 (Minneapolis, 1897), in MPL-SC.

10. *The Attic Club Yearbook 1924–1925* (Minneapolis, 1924?); includes a history and membership information; in MPL-SC together with the club's record books, letters, and memorabilia.

11. Information on these organizations is largely from the files on them in MPL-SC.

12. Kay V. Spangler, *Survey of Serial Fine Art Exhibitions and Artists in Minnesota 1900–1970,* I-II (St. Paul, 1997).

13. Rena Coen, *Painting and Sculpture in Minnesota, 1820–1914* (Minneapolis, 1976), 46,67.

14. Donald Torbert, *A Century of Art and Architecture in Minnesota* (Minneapolis, 1958), 17–18.

15. Catalogue at MHS.

16. *Accomplishments: Minnesota Art Projects in the Depression,* a small exhibition catalogue (Minneapolis, n.d.), 4–10. Newspaper coverage relating to specific artists.

17. *Accomplishments,* 4–5, 9–10.

18. Odd S. Lovoll, *The Promise of America* (Minneapolis, 1984), 27.

19. Lovoll, *The Promise of America,* 12, 15–16.

20. According to the catalogues of the expositions, the Society exhibited a collection of Melvold studies in 1888 and eight Melvold works in 1893, both after the death of the artist.

21. Spangler, *Survey.*

22. The painting is a view of Rjukan Valley from the Torgrim farm in Norway and was done for the Torgrim family near Decorah, IA. Now at Vesterheim.

23. Marion Nelson, *Norway to America* (Decorah, IA, 1989), 54–64; the Chicago painters of Norwegian subjects are dealt with in some detail.

24. It was deaccessioned in 1991 and attempts to trace its whereabouts have failed.

Illustrations

Norway and the Sea

Most of the early immigrant artists who were trained before arrival continued for a time to paint the subjects familiar from home. The difficulty they had finding patrons for specifically Norwegian works indicates that the immigrants were either not culturally or economically ready for original art or they wanted something more representative of their new life.

1. Peter Lund. *Shipwreck*. Oil. ca 1890. 12 x 18. Tweed Museum of Art, University of Minnesota, Duluth, MN, Gift of George H. Crosby Estate.

Lund may have been the first Norwegian-American artist active in Minnesota, exhibiting in Minneapolis from 1883 and spending four years in Duluth after 1893. The "may" is because his origin has not been documented. He could have been Danish.

2. Peter Lund. *Sailboat off Lighthouse.* Oil. ca 1890. 26 x 18. Tweed Museum of Art, Crosby Estate.

The subtle handling of light and the bold composition of this painting, and the delicacy of brushwork in *Shipwreck* indicate that Lund had academic training.

4. Haakon Melvold. *Rena River in Norway.* Oil. 1871. 12 x 18. Minnesota Historical Society.

Melvold painted this scene from his home area near Hamar when in Chicago a year after leaving Norway. It has the detailed depiction of nature typical of his Dusseldorf-trained teacher J. F. Eckersberg. Melvold returned to Norway the same year this work was painted.

5. Haakon Melvold. *Waterfall in Gudbrandsdalen, Norway.* (Opposite) Oil. 1887. 43 x 34. Clark and Karen Lyda.

In 1883 Melvold came back, now settling in Minneapolis where he painted exclusively Norwegian scenes and found few buyers. This large work is apparently the one with the above title exhibited in 1887. The following year Melvold died in total poverty.

3. Carl L. Boeckmann. *The Pilot.* Oil. ca 1910. 30 x 25. Vesterheim, Decorah, IA, Gift of Lloyd and Betty LeDell.

Sea pilots are one Norwegian subject that must have found buyers because Boeckmann painted many. Some became routine and tightly executed but this one has the freshness of the sea itself.

6. Herbjorn Gausta. *From Breivik.* Oil. ca 1890. 19 x 28. Luther College, Decorah, IA.

Gausta emigrated before going back to study art in Oslo and Germany. In Munich he picked up the brighter colors and broader brushstrokes of the Naturalists, quite different from those of Melvold. He had family in Telemark where the south coastal town of Breivik is located.

7. Herbjorn Gausta. *Young Mother.* Oil. ca 1890. 19 x 28. Luther College.

The setting appears to be Gardjord, Rauland, Telemark, where Gausta's family on his mother's side lived. His early Munich training was in figure painting which, except for altar pieces and portraits, he soon gave up for landscapes.

8. Herbjorn Gausta. *Summertime* (The Haymakers). Oil. 1882. 15 x 20. Luther College.

A study for this painting is in a sketchbook, apparently from 1881 when Gausta was in Rauland. He is just developing landscape painting and uses the fresh green colors of modern French painters exhibited in Munich in 1879.

Rural Life and Landscape

Most first and second generation artists of Norwegian background came from farms, and landscape had been the most prevalent type of painting in Norway since the early 19th century. It is therefore natural to find rural life and landscape dominating Norwegian immigrant art.

9. Herbjorn Gausta. *Washington Prairie Parsonage* (exterior). Oil. 1883. 10 x 15. Vesterheim, Gift of Elsa Naeseth Estate.

Having been exposed in Europe to painting on the site, Gausta made the change from Norwegian to American subject matter with ease. He was often a guest of his benefactors, Reverend and Mrs. U. V. Koren, at this parsonage and he gives it an air of gentility characteristic of their lives in Norway.

10. Herbjorn Gausta. *Washington Prairie Parsonage* (interior). Oil. 1883 (?). 10 x 14. Vesterheim, Gift of Mary Elizabeth Naeseth Estate.

The pastor's study has an American air. The simple Norwegian-style log chair on the right, probably made for him at the time of his arrival twenty years earlier, is the only obvious Norwegian touch.

11. Charles Thoresen. *Landscape.* Oil. ca 1900. 9 x 12. Dennis and Rosemari Anderson.

After the late 1880s, Thoresen did not exhibit, so he must have done his small landscapes only as studies for panels in decorative schemes. His balanced composition and subtle color are exceptional.

12. Orabel Thortvedt. *Dog.* Pastel. 1941. 13 x 16. Eva and Carl Hedstrom.

Thortvedt was not, like Thoresen, a decorator, but she brought decorative qualities into her work as seen in the handling of the coat on this cocker spaniel. A farm woman, she felt close to animals and portrayed them with character.

13. Orabel Thortvedt. *Ola G. Thortveidt.* (Opposite) Oil. 1938. ca 42 x 36. Eva and Carl Hedstrom.

Next to animals, Thortvedt's obsession was her grandfather Ola Thortveidt, who led a caravan of Norwegian immigrants from Houston county in southern Minnesota to the Buffalo River east of Moorhead. She paints him as the patriarch he was, but ready to take her in his lap. Behind him is the Houston county he left.

14. Orabel Thortvedt. *Gamle Joran.* Ink. ca 1930s. 10 x 8. Eva and Carl Hedstrom.

Ola's mother Joran, already a grandmother, had crossed the Atlantic in 1861 and had also made the trek north. Orabel would not have seen her but created an image more telling than a photograph.

15. Orabel Thortvedt. *The Caravan Halts for Night Camp.* Ink. ca 1930s. 10 x 12. Eva and Carl Hedstrom.

The uneasiness of the animals as the caravan halts in the darkness reveals Orabel's keen understanding of them.

Portrait of Grandpa, Olav G. Thortvedt

16. Margit Mindrum. *Spring Plowing.* Gouache. 1960. 15 x 19. Frieda and Ron Nowland.

Mindrum gives us the Houston county that the Thortvedts left. Like Orabel, Margit knew the farm. Her spring is loaded with the fragrance of apple blossoms and the earth exposed by plowing.

17. Margit Mindrum. *Haying.* Gouache. 1971. 16 x 28. Stanley and Janet Oian.

The yellow that breaks through the green, and the haze in the air convey the heat associated with haying. The southeast Minnesota terrain is masterfully depicted.

18. Margit Mindrum. *Farm Corn Shocks.* Gouache. 1963. 16 x 20. Sonja Genett.

A photograph could have been the model for this exceptional Minnesota landscape, but Mindrum never copied exactly. The qualities that make this *art* come undoubtedly from her.

19. Margit Mindrum. *Winter Scene, Cutter.* Gouache. 1971. 11 x 20. Ruby and Herb Highum.

As in Ill. 16, Mindrum has loaded her scene with characteristics of the season, masses of snow and a low hazy sun. "Winter seems like a dream," she said and she gives it a dream like character, including a cutter probably no longer in use.

20. Axel E. Schar. *Logging Drive on River* (one of four panels on the industries of Duluth). Oil. ca 1940. 86 x 40. St. Louis County Historical Society. (Photographed before restoration.)

Seascapes and landscapes were Schar's forte, but here figures join the energy of the water and the movement of the logs.

21. Lloyd Herfindahl. *Captive.* (Opposite) Acrylic. ca 1968. 18 x 24. Minnesota Historical Society.

The artist gives a penetrating view of the lonely and trapped life of the pioneer woman. She looks out on a world from which she is kept back by an actual fence and also a phantom fence in the form of a shadow.

22. Lloyd Herfindahl. *Threshing Time* (in the *County Fair* series). (Opposite) Watercolor. ca 1955. 18 x 23. Minnesota Historical Society.

While often presenting rural life from an ideal standpoint, Herfindahl here gives us the greed and vulgarity that can develop among people whose lives are bound to eking out a living from the soil.

42

23. Mathias (Matt) Wolden. *Meadow in Bloom.* Oil. ca 1930. 10 x 12. Vesterheim.

We have seen *life* in the country, but many painters were more interested in the landscape itself. Wolden was the poet among them though earning his living through day labor in Duluth.

24. Olaf Aalbu, Sr. *Winter River.* (Opposite) Oil. 1920s. 32 x 27. Vesterheim, Gift of Jeanette Aalbu.

While primarily a decorator, Aalbu too could be a poet. This view of what is probably Minnehaha Creek has an Impressionist quality because the yellow in bits of the exposed canvas complements the painted blue.

25. Arnold Klagstad. *Ilgen Falls* (North Shore). Oil. 1940. 18 x 22. Vesterheim.

Usually a painter of the city (Ill. 33), Klagstad also did landscapes. The influence of Cezanne is seen in the faceting of the rocks and the even filling of the frame.

26. Carl Olderen. *Golden Valley Farm.* Oil. 1930. 24 x 28. Arling and Lois Olderen.

Olderen literally brings the cubes, spheres, and cones of Cezanne into this farm scene, which together with its rather bright colors sets it apart from much of his work (Ill. 35). He too was generally a painter of the city.

27. Einar Dahl. *Mystic Hollow* (Mazeppa, MN). Oil. 1941 (later rendition of a work from 1939). 24 x 30. Robbinsdale Historical Society.

This is an unusual work by a largely self-trained artist experimenting with making line and color function apart from representing nature. Dahl's earlier version was in American Art Today at the New York World's Fair in 1940.

28. John Maakestad. *Spring Landscape.* Oil. 1956. 25 x 28. Edward and Genevieve Sovik.

Maakestad approaches abstraction differently from Dahl, breaking down the elements of his subject into small geometric units, sometimes brushstrokes, which from a distance come together to create the image.

29. Charles Beck. *Warm Winter.* Oil. 1960. 36 x 53. U.S. Bank, Minneapolis, MN.

Beck, like Maakestad, has an MFA from the University of Iowa and has a similar approach to landscape although departing less from nature's actual forms. Both, like Mindrum, Dahl and Olderen (Ill. 16–19, 26, 27), explore the specific character of the Minnesota countryside.

The City

While the rural origins of many of our artists are directly reflected in much of their work, an attraction of opposites also gave the city appeal to them, with Arnold Klagstad (Ill. 33) making it a specialty.

30. Charles Thoresen. *Corner of 1st Street and 5th Avenue, Duluth.* Pencil. June 6, 1890. 5 x 7. Dennis and Rosemari Anderson.

The city enters indirectly into Thoresen's work, appearing only in sketchbook drawings, perhaps made for pleasure rather than as studies for larger works. His mastery of perspective and keen observation of detail make them special in Minnesota art of 1890.

31. Magnus Norstad. *City on a Hill.* (Opposite) Oil. 1917. 36 x 30. Minnesota Historical Society.

The most lyrical cityscape known from the Twin Cities, this depiction of St. Paul won both a People's Choice Award and a Silver Medal there in 1917. Three years later the artist left for New York and did not return.

32. Sverre Hanssen. *Train Yard* (St. Paul). Oil. ca 1940. 33 x 42. Ah-Gwah-Ching Historical Society.

Like Norstad's St. Paul, Hanssen's gets some of its effectiveness from showing the city both as a metropolis on the river and a railroad center. While lacking the delicate brushwork of the Norstad, this painting is in spite of its precise execution marvelously atmospheric.

33. Arnold Klagstad. *Washington—Crosby Elevator.* Oil. 1934. 33 x 40. Minneapolis Public Library.

For Klagstad grain elevators were the hallmark of the city. They bring Charles Sheeler to mind but, unlike him, Klagstad includes elements of the natural setting in his work. A related Klagstad was purchased by the Metropolitan Museum in New York but has since been deaccessioned.

34. Cyrus Running. *Urban Renewal #4.* Oil. 1965. 28 x 47. Moorhead Public Library.

Running, who like Maakestad (Ill. 28) and Beck (Ill. 29) has an MFA from Iowa, originally painted rural Minnesota but was increasingly drawn to cities. This impeccable composition explores the pictorial in urban renewal without making judgment.

57

35. Carl Olderen. *River Flats in Winter.* Oil. 1930. 24 x 28. Arling and Lois Olderen.

Urban renewal would not have been looked on with favor by Olderen, who found that the cubes and slopping roofs of the closely placed squatter houses under Washington Avenue Bridge related perfectly to his love of faceted forms.

37. Olaf Aalbu, Jr. *Courtyard, Paris.* (Opposite) Oil. 1946. 26 x 21. Vesterheim.

The young Aalbu, like Grinager, was studying in Paris when he discovered this courtyard near the Odeon Metro Station. The French too must have liked it because his painting was interrupted by a movie crew getting shots for a film.

36. Alexander Grinager. *Grand Canal, Venice.* Oil. 1894. 20 x 15. Vesterheim.

It was naturally the old and the quaint that appealed to American art students in Europe because it was different from home. On the Grand Canal, Grinager was also able to experiment with an Impressionist approach to light that he would apply later the same year in *Boys Bathing* (Ill. 44).

Hard Times

War and the Depression were the major causes of the hard times reflected in immigrant art. Curiously, the German occupation of Norway, 1940–1945, left no known mark in art here while it resulted in several powerful works in the Norwegian colony of Brooklyn. The greater distance from Norway and the earlier immigration here may have accounted for this.

38. Carl L. Boeckmann. *Col. Hans C. Heg and the 15th Wisconsin at Chickamauga, 1863.* Oil. ca 1915. 29 x 36. Charles Holt.

This is an amazingly straightforward presentation of an historic battle. Col. Heg, who lost his life here, is mounted but not otherwise glorified. Considered a sketch, no further commission came. A commercial print was made.

39. Sydney Fossum. *The Meeting.* Oil. 1937. 36 x 48. Minnesota Historical Society.

Fossum was an agitator for social justice. It is characteristic that this meeting of the disadvantaged during the Depression includes women and men, young and old, black and white. His completely sincere characterizations reflect his deep compassion.

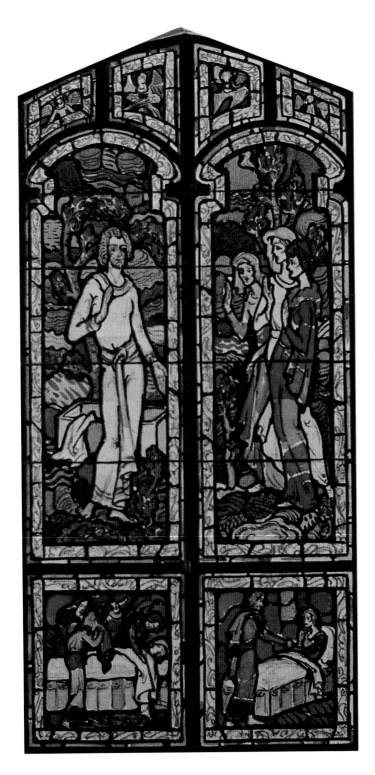

Celebration

Norwegian-American celebration art is almost exclusively related to the church. Norwegian and immigrant national holidays have left no significant mark in painting. The celebration of the ethnic has been limited almost exclusively to sculpture and revived folk arts.

40. Andreas R. Larsen. *Resurrection.* Watercolor. ca 1930. 9 x 4. Minneapolis Public Library, Special Collections.

Larsen was an exhibiting artist as well as a stained glass designer and producer but only his work relating to these are known. His *Resurrection* has a turn-of-the-century modernity unusual in his work.

41. John Anderson. *Christmas* (panel 4 of 4). (Opposite) Oil. 1970. 48 x 36. Dr. and Mrs. Malcolm. A. McCannel.

Christmas dominated celebration in Norway, bringing light in a season of darkness. It retains prominence among Norwegian Americans as a time when ethnic customs, especially in food, are momentarily revived. There is nothing ethnic about Anderson's tree, but it is a wonderful expression of childish delight from only months before his death.

People as People

Figure painting was never strong in Norwegian art, and it has few strong representatives in the immigrant art of Minnesota. The altarpieces are almost invariably copies of European models, and the most productive portraitist, August Klagstad, worked primarily from photographs. But delightful examples exist.

42. Herbjorn Gausta. *The Secret.* Oil. 1884. 28 x 22. Steensland Art Museum, St. Olaf College.

Paintings of touching human actions were popular in Germany where Gausta studied. In this American work done not long after his return, he used a cousin as the model for the girl on the right and Professor Gisle Bothne's daughter Anna for the girl telling the secret. Bothne, then at Luther College, was later at the University of Minnesota.

43. Carl L. Boeckmann. *Family Reading the Minneapolis Journal.* Oil. 1915. 24 x 36. Marilyn Boeckmann Anderson.

This painting of family life, rare in Norwegian-American art, was probably done on the occasion of settling into the new house which the Boeckmanns are known to have gotten this year. It is a charming blend of the casual and the formal.

44. Alexander Grinager. *Boys Bathing.* Oil. 1894. 34 x 59. Minneapolis Institute of Arts.

Grinager was probably the most versatile figure painter of our group, but his great figurative murals are gone. His boys bathing under Washington Avenue Bridge near the flats (see also Ill. 35) are like studies of the body in various positions.

45. J. Theodore Sohner. *Mrs. Otto Iverson Brack.* Oil. 1932. 36 x 30. Vesterheim, Gift of Norse-American Centennial Daughters through Ione Kadden.

A prominent figure in the cultural life of the Twin Cities, Mrs. Brack was also the artist's aunt. The profile view is simple but exceedingly effective, especially with the decorative textile background.

46. J. Theodore Sohner. *Ione Brack.* Oil. March 6, 1928. 24 x 18. Ione Brack Kadden.

The artist painted his cousin Ione four years before the mother. He was 22 and just beginning portraiture, but he gave the work a tenderness that covers any lack of experience. Ione assumed her mother's prominence in the cultural life of the Twin Cities.

47. Peter Teigen. *Young Man in Kimono.* Oil. ca 1935. 34 x 27. Vesterheim.

An Associate Professor at Princeton when he died at 41, Teigen rose faster in the art world than any other painter in our group. He began as the son of an immigrant family in north Minneapolis. The subtlety of the light and perfection of the composition in this work attest to his exceptional ability.

Art as Art

Because of Edvard Munch, Norwegian art is often associated with intense expression. In general, however, it tends more toward the formal. This is true of Minnesota Norwegian immigrant art as well. Line, color, texture, and composition can constitute the major interest of the work.

48. Olaf Aalbu, Sr. *Sun Flowers.* Oil. ca 1925. 32 x 12. Jeannette Aalbu.

The artist in our group who had the greatest potential for significant development beyond his 47 years is Olaf Aalbu, Sr. The diversity of vision between *Winter River* (Ill. 24) and this work, both completely developed statements, is exceptional in Minnesota painting of the early 1920s.

49. Elmar Berge. *Peonies.* Oil. ca. 1950s. 20 x 26. Vesterheim, Gift of Esther Peterson.

Form as such is probably less important for Berge than for any other of our artists, but some of his best paintings are floral still lifes in which the decorative becomes one with the subject. The brush strokes themselves in this work are a part of its language.

50. August Klagstad. *Still Life.* Oil. ca. 1931. 20 x 16. Vesterheim.

August Klagstad's still lifes and landscapes show a strong element of Cezanne that is completely absent in his altar pieces and most of his portraits. Works like this one throw new light on an artist generally considered academic.

51. Einar Dahl. *Basic Forms.* Oil. 1961 (later rendition of painting from 1939). 27 x 37. Jan and John Kordash and John Kordash Jr.

Abstractions in Dahl's work go back to the late 1930s when he was trying to find the right form for *Mystic Valley* (Ill. 27). Although uneven, the best abstractions become sheer poetry through the spatial ambiguities in their intersecting planes of color and texture. To Dahl they spoke an inner language, the subconscious made conscious.

Stories of the Artists

For the sake of brevity, years in this section are often reduced to the last two digits where there can be no ambiguity regarding the century. For simplicity, the sources of information on each artist are given at the end of this section rather than in footnotes.

OLAF AALBU, JR. b. 1917
Illustration 37

It was a great loss to Norwegian-American painting that Olaf H. Aalbu, son of the artist by the same name, was drawn away from art in the 1960s when recalled into military service to work on the Titan Missile Program and finally the completion of the eighteen Missile Sites Project near Tucson. With this completed, he stayed in the west to work for Douglas (later McDonnell Douglas) Aircraft Manufacturing Company until his retirement in 1983. The pressure in these positions forced him more and more away from art, his one-man exhibition at the Millionaires Club in Tucson around the late 1960s being apparently his last.

The length and breadth of Aalbu's exposure to and training in art exceeds that of any artist in our group, and there is evidence of both great dedication and innate ability. He was born in Minneapolis September 17, 1917, to parents from outside Trondheim, Norway. His mother too was an artist, having both studied and taught tapestry weaving as a young woman. Already at the age of six Olaf did competitive drawing with his brothers on the back of a twelve-foot long roll of wallpaper hung horizontally in their bedroom. At about the same time he got a first prize at school for a drawing of a Viking ship. Knowing the economic struggles of the father, his mother did not encourage the son to work with him, but the young Olaf took a correspondence course in art and studied with the excellent artist Alexander Masley (b.1903) at the Minneapolis School of Art. When the WPA Art Center in the Sexton Building opened in the mid 1930s, he worked with the very best of the young graduates from the School of Art: Mac LeSueur (b. 1908), Syd Fossum, Elof Wedin (1901–1983), and Erle Loran (1908–1998). He had an oil portrait admitted to the 23rd Annual Twin City Art Exhibit at the Minneapolis Institute of Arts in 1937, and the following year got the first award on a drawing called *Shelter Shocked,* also at the Institute. He was then 21 years old. Already the previous year his colleagues had wanted him in the Artists Union but had to give him honorary membership because of his being under age. He exhibited again at the Institute in 1939 and got a second award on his print *Roustabouts Resting.* Several years later he was called into service; but already in 1946 he was back exhibiting at the Institute's Twin City Art Exhibit.

Aalbu had traumatic war experiences, being in Germany to see the opening of the concentration and prisoner of war camps. He felt that he must use his art to leave a record of what he saw; but on being taken to Norway by an uncle shortly later, he found artists who had been actually in these camps painting landscapes as if nothing had happened. Hans Ryggen, husband of Norway's renowned tapestry artist Hannah Ryggen, was his greatest inspiration in learning to forget the past and look to the future. Several of Aalbu's paintings were admitted to the fall exhibition in Trondheim and received favorable critiques.

The GI bill brought Aalbu to Paris early in 1948 where his best known teachers at the Grand Chaumiere were Othan Friesz (1879–1949) in painting and Ossip Zadkine (1890–1967) in sculpture. He married the French Irene Coudert in 1949 and continued to study at the Ecole des Beaux-Arts. His work was now admitted to the Salon d'Automne at the Petit Palais, where John Anderson also exhibited, and again critiques were good. He was included in the American Painters in France exhibition as well. In 1950 he was again at the Minneapolis Institute of Arts with two lithographs, apparently sent from Paris, and got a third prize. Opportunities to exhibit continued to come, but funds ran out and he took jobs in France, Morocco, and Spain until returning to the United States in 1960. Before being called back into service, Aalbu exhibited again at the Institute in 1960 and at the Duluth Art Institute's invitational in 1962. His last major solo show in the Midwest was a retrospective at the Art Works Gallery in the Tonka Terrace Shopping Center, Excelsior, in 1960. His one earlier solo exhibition here had been at the Rainbow Cafe in the late forties and consisted only of lithographs.

Drawing, printmaking, and painting played almost equally in Aalbu's work. He did his first printmaking on salvaged equipment that he learned to operate himself, but he gained enough expertise to get a second award at the Institute in 1939. Later he brought his printmaking to a very high level in Paris. His style in all media is basically realistic but tends toward the curvilinear and expressionistic. *Courtyard, Paris* (Ill.37) is a modest and unusually serene example.

OLAF HERMAN AALBU, SR. 1878–1926
Illustrations 24, 48

Olaf Herman Aalbu was born to Sivert and Henrietta Aalbu on Broholm, Ørland, Sør Trøndelag, August 8, 1878. An improperly healed leg broken in a fall from a rocky outcropping probably led to his being released from farm work and allowed to study voice, violin, and art at the art school in Trondheim. In 1902 he came to Minneapolis where his brother Oscar was established as a saloon keeper and where his art teacher from Trondheim, Einar Ofstie, had been active ten years earlier. Here he married Gurine Bakken from Bjugn, Sør Trøndelag, who had been a professional weaver in Norway. In 1907 he made a return visit to Norway with the Dovre Singing Society.

Although music was Aalbu's primary interest at the time of immigration, he was employed as a painter already in 1903 by the prestigious decorating firm of John S. Bradstreet. Later he appears to have also done free-lance work but was with the Smith-Larson Decorative Company in 1905 and back with Bradstreet in 1914. Among the Minneapolis buildings in which Aalbu is reported to have been centrally involved as a decorator are the Commercial and University clubs, the Metropolitan Opera, the Knights of Columbus Hall, the Courthouse (a courtroom ceiling which has now been repainted), the old Radisson Hotel, and the Great Northern Depot.

While listed in the Minneapolis Directory first as a painter, then from 1906 as a decorator, and only in his late years as an artist, Aalbu was a prolific easel painter all his life. When asked by a reporter from *Minneapolis Tidende* in 1912 why he did not exhibit, he said he was afraid his work could have artistic and technical flaws and that he hated to ask for the assistance he would need in exhibiting. The final response was that he would rather paint.

Perhaps encouraged by the interview, his works appeared at the annual exhibitions sponsored by the Minnesota State Art Society and later the State Fair in 1913–14, 25, and at the Minneapolis Institute of Arts in 1923. For three consecutive years from 1920 he also participated in the exhibitions of the Norwegian Club in Chicago. The family recalled awards but record of these has not been found. While he had two works at the State Fair exhibition in the fall of 1925, he is conspicuously absent from the Norse Centennial Exhibition on the same grounds in June of that year. On January 23 the following year Aalbu died at age 47 of tuberculosis, a disease that claimed many members of his family.

Existing works, now largely at Vesterheim, indicate that Aalbu's early style was primitively flat and linear but acquired a finely-nuanced academic character during his early years in America. Looser brush strokes and a tendency toward unusual color and light effects developed in the teens and led by about 1920 to a mosaic-like quality in the application of paint and a highly decorative use of line. Although relating to Van Gogh, the style is advanced and stands alone in Minnesota painting of the early 1920s (Ill. 48). I assume it was this late approach to painting that gave the mammoth Glacier Park scene in the Great Northern Depot, which I vaguely recall, its vibrant character.

As to subject matter, Aalbu's very early work included landscapes from Norway, but these soon gave way to painting the family members both indoors and out, scenes in parks both summer and winter, and finally floral still lifes. Most of his work is restful and represents a positive view of life. An apparent exception to this is *The Sinking of the Titanic*, a four by six foot canvas completed within two weeks of the April 14–15, 1912, disaster. A journalist reports on May 5 that he finds the subject quite unlike Aalbu but considers the painting a sincere reflection of the artist's own experience with the sea as an immigrant from coastal Norway. It was shown at the annual exhibit of the Minnesota State Art Society the following year, but its later history is unknown.

The early death of Aalbu was a great loss to Norwegian-American painting in Minneapolis. It is generally conservative, but Aalbu developed rapidly in style and largely on the bases of his own experimentations. One wonders where he might have gone from *Sunflowers* (Ill. 48), which is probably the work exhibited as *Flowers* in 1925, the year before his death. A still life from this period is in the same technique but is far more complex in composition and surface pattern.

JOHN E. ANDERSON 1923–1971
Illustration 41

Only two of the artists presented here are known to have some non-Norwegian background. John E. Anderson has the most, with a German mother, Clara Schumacher Anderson, from Mankato, Minnesota. John was born there on August 10, 1923, but he soon moved with his parents to Huron, South Dakota. His father Elmer had come from South Dakota where the family had a furniture and funeral business in Canton. The boy was named after his grandfather, John Anderson, who had emigrated from Mosjøen in North Norway and founded the business in the late 19th century.

In Huron, where John lived through his high school years, the family had a floral shop which has been mentioned as an explanation for the frequency with which plants and flowers appear in his work. He had early exposure to the arts through an aunt, Palma Anderson, an accomplished pianist trained in Germany. The texture, harmony, and line of music remained important in his visual work. When asked about his favorite artists in 1951, he listed along with the painters Giotto (ca 1266–ca 1337), Paul Klee (1879–1940), and Ben Nicholson (1894–1982), the musicians Bach, Beethoven, Mozart, Billie Holliday, and Satchmo. Art work also began in Huron, as evidenced by an oil with a vase of flowers dated 1941.

John was at South Dakota State University, Aberdeen, in 1943 when he was drafted into the U.S. Army and became a demolition expert who was parachuted into France before D-Day. His war experience, according to Bruce Rubenstein, "left Anderson with a liberation attitude toward life,…a witty, manic personality with eyes that burned with humor and intelligence." He gradually lost his handle on life but kept his art firmly in order.

After his discharge in 1945 Anderson completed two years of study and also taught at the Walker Art School in Minneapolis with Mac LeSueur as a mentor. Study continued for two years under the GI bill at the Academie de la Grande Chaumiere in Paris. Here, as later during stays in New York from 1950 to 1952 and 1958 to 1959, Anderson was accepted by prestigious galleries and included in major exhibitions. Museums in which his work appeared with other top young artists of the time included the Musee d'Art Moderne in Paris and the Whitney and Guggenheim in New York. The Hacker Gallery of that city and the Kilbride-Bradley Gallery of Minneapolis took special interest in Anderson and gave him several solo exhibitions in addition to carrying his work regularly. He continued through the rest of his life to exhibit extensively in the Twin Cities, and during the early fifties won several firsts and many other prizes in addition to purchase awards at both the Minneapolis Institute of Arts and the Walker Art Center.

Sales were more limited than recognition. For income Anderson taught at the Colorado Springs Fine Arts Center, 1952–53, and the University of Minnesota Extension, 1954–56. From 1953 to 1957 he was also an exhibition assistant at the Walker Art Center. Declining health and sales together with increasing alcoholism led to his leaving urban life in 1960 for Battle Lake, Minnesota, where his wife, who was originally from that area, and their five children had settled two years earlier. He continued to paint and occasionally to exhibit until his death at age 47, June 3, 1971.

The memorial service was held in the local Norwegian Lutheran Church but with a Catholic priest who was his friend also participating. His completely Norwegian wife Elenore Rowe had strengthened his contact with his father's background. The closeness is reflected in the names of his children: Stener, Kristi, Breda, Lisa, and Karl. The immigrant community recognized him and he it through an exhibition at the Sons of Norway Building in 1962.

With or without a recognizable subject, Anderson's paintings contain a dialogue between space and mass, the finite and the infinite. His use of texture as well as color in his visual language brings Paul Klee to mind, but he was never directly imitative of other's work. He was an avid reader who as a teenager is said to have read half the *Encyclopedia Britannica* when housebound with a broken leg. Words apart from specific meaning can also find a place in his painting, as seen in *Christmas* (Ill. 41). He came nearer genius than any Minnesota painter of Norwegian background. Few of his works are now on display in museums, but he is being seen perhaps more than any other Minnesota artist through his six by forty-eight foot mural, *Carousel*, commissioned by the Dayton Company in 1956 and now in the Garden Court at Brookdale Shopping Center.

CHARLES NELSON BECK b. 1923
Illustration 29

There is scarcely a Minnesota artist who is a more integral part of the Norwegian immigrant community than Charles Beck. He was born January 31, 1923, in Fergus Falls at the heart of a large rural area running south to Alexandria, east to Detroit Lakes, north through the Red River Valley and west into northeastern North Dakota that is heavily settled with immigrants from Norway. Most of his background is also Norwegian, with the major line going back to Hedemark. One-fourth of his background is Swedish. The area of his birth, where he is still active and has spent all but a few years of his life, also has a common geographic character, although the rolling and partially wooded hills of the southeastern part level off and become largely bare to the north and west. It is this landscape, so intimately associated with rural Norwegian immigrant life, that "Charlie" Beck has taught us all to see.

Beck's approach to his environment is not sentimental; it might rather be called intellectual. The works, however, still have mood, often conveying an air of loneliness. The marks of man are almost always present in the division of fields and the parallel lines of furrows or planted crops, but the doer is usually absent. One stands instead confronted with a divine presence suggested by the vastness of the views, the ever-present sky, or the sheer order of things.

Beck's training is as rooted in his community as his vision is in his environment. His first mentor in art was Cyrus Running, presented elsewhere here, whose base in Norwegian Minnesota culture was even greater than Beck's. They met at Concordia College, Moorhead, where Beck received his B.A. in 1948. He continued to follow his mentor's footsteps by going for advanced study to the University of Iowa, an institution which at mid-century left a strong mark on art in the Norwegian Lutheran colleges of the upper midwest. An example is *Spring Landscape* (Ill. 28), a work quite similar to Beck's *Warm Winter* (Ill. 29), by John Maakestad, whose background and affiliation was St. Olaf College but who also had an MFA from Iowa. Again following his mentor, Beck in 1957 studied at San Miguel Allende in Mexico, an experience that may have deepened his respect for the life and spirituality of so-called "primitive" peoples. This is very evident in his mural *Native American Life* (1956) in Pennington County Court House, Thief River Falls, Minnesota, and in a group of atypical watercolors done of native life in Madagascar in 1978.

Unlike a number of artists in the northern area of Minnesota, Charles Beck has had close affiliation with the art scene in the Twin Cities. In the winter of 1953 he took art courses at the University of Minnesota, where he was in contact with Cameron Booth and Walter Quirt, and where Malcolm Myer was an inspiration in his development of the woodcut, a medium that has been central in his late work. He exhibited at the State Fair in 1951–54, 56–62, and 64, receiving in 1951, first in oils; 1952, third in oils; 1957, first on two watercolors; 1958, second in oils and drawings; 1959, third in both casein and prints; 1960, first in oils, second in watercolors, and third in drawings; 1961, first in watercolors, third in prints. At the Minneapolis Institute of Arts he exhibited only in 1959, 61, and 63, receiving an Honorable Mention in oils in 1959, and at the Walker Art Center only in 1956 and 62. After 1960 much of his exhibiting shifted to the Red River Annual Art Exhibitions in Moorhead where he participated in 1960 and 62–68, receiving in 1960 and 62 Honorable Mention in oils, in 1964 and 65 Merit Award in oils, and in 67 a Collectors Purchase Award. He has had one-man shows, some invitational as part of larger exhibitions, at the Harriet Hanley Gallery (1954), the Walker Art Center (1956), and the Minneapolis Institute of Arts (1962) in Minneapolis and at Bethel College (1956), the Minnesota State Fair (1960), Kramer Gallery (1967), the Public Library (1974), and the Suzanne Kohn Gallery (1977) in St. Paul.

The concentration of Beck's activities in general since the early sixties has been in his home area. He has contributed much to building up the Ottertail County Historical Society in Fergus Falls and creating its dioramas; and he has taught art on a part-time basis at the Fergus Falls Community College. The collecting and carving of decoys is a major hobby, and art-making continues, largely in the form of highly stylized but lyrical and delicately carved color woodcuts.

ELMAR S. BERGE 1893–1956
Illustartion 44

Of Minnesota artists with Norwegian background, Elmar Berge was the most romantic both in disposition and painting style. A bachelor, he wrote to a female friend when he was 62 years old, "I like all that is light and gay." He was born on the island of Finnø off the Norwegian coast near Stavanger, in 1893. He emigrated in 1914. Seven years later he graduated from Pleasant View Luther College (actually a Lutheran academy offering a high school education). He may have chosen the location because of Berge families in the area who are assumed to have been relatives. Learning English may have been his motivation for his enrolling since he was about ten years older than most of the students.

The 1920s finds Berge in Chicago where his career as an artist may have begun. He is said to have worked with the English painter Sir Matthew William Thompson (1872–1956) when he was painting on the west coast of Norway, but fellow students at Pleasant View Lutheran did not recall his being associated with art there. In Chicago he studied with James W. McBurney (b. 1868) at the Art Institute and learned also from his personal association with the Swedish-American marine painter Leon Lundmark (b. 1875) and the Norwegian-American Gulbrand Saether (1869–1941). Already in 1926 he was exhibiting at the Norwegian Club of Chicago and had work accepted there again in 1929 and 30. The following year he played a role in organizing the Norse Art League, which attempted to continue the Norwegian Club exhibits, but in 1932 he appears as an artist in the Minneapolis City Directory. Minneapolis remained his home until his death in early April, 1956.

Berge never entered juried exhibitions in the Twin Cities. He apparently felt uncomfortable outside the Norwegian-American art circle that had embraced him in Chicago. Being economically dependent on his art, he also had to paint for sale rather than for winning prizes. He also seems to have enjoyed most just getting the direct impulses from nature and capturing the scene in his own manner; and he did have a manner. It consisted of rather broad feathery brush strokes and a composition with strong foreground elements that opened in the middle or on one side to reveal a distant vista. A stream, lake, or road served as a link between the two. In landscapes he had a predilection for autumn colors with contrasting blue in the sky and water. In seascapes, which are less common, blue can dominate.

Floral still lifes did not allow this formula to be applied and are therefore among his most distinctive works, but they are also few (Ill. 29). In them the energy of the brush strokes conveys some of the energy of nature itself held captive in the bouquet. In fact, the best of his landscapes are those in which the entire surface has been energized by brush strokes as in the landscapes of Gainsborough. Occasional early examples get their distinction through a coloration so artificial that they seem more symbolic than real. This can also occur in Gulbrand Sether's work which occasionally takes on the character of the now highly regarded "symbolic landscapes" of turn-of-the-century Scandinavian artists.

Berge may have sold as many paintings to special admirers as to the general public. Among these were Marge Dockerty of Rochester, where he had two one-man exhibitions in 1947. About 65 works from her collection were sold at auction in 1998. Vi Osteberg of Minneapolis is said to have had paintings, probably not in the same numbers. He may also have had the patronage of the collector Lyman Johnson, who was a personal friend. His major outlet in Minneapolis is said to have been a downtown art store owned by Joseph Zesbough.

In spite of the hand-to-mouth existence reported by acquaintances, Berge made several trips to Europe, not only to Norway, but to England, Scotland, France, Italy, and Austria. His romantic disposition seems to have kept him above the realities of existence on a meagre income. Writing from his home farm on Finnø at 62, he says, "I have heard the cuckoo bird . . . many memories were awakened and like a boy again I laid down in the grass and dreamt away." He continues, "Next month I shall set sail for the blue Mediterranean to drink in its wine and music." But perhaps he was getting tired. Toward the end of the letter he says, "The more I travel...the more I appreciate America." Within nine months he was dead.

CARL LUDWIG BOECKMANN 1867–1923
Illustrations 3, 38, 43

Carl Boeckmann was what one expects an artist in an immigrant community to be. His dress and demeanor set him apart so that both his countrymen and established Americans knew that here was an artist of the old school. "Wearing a fiery red beard and a carefully kept moustache, a flowing tie and clothes in keeping, Mr. Boeckmann presented the figure of a man just stepped out of the Latin quarter." This is how he was described in his obituary in *The Minneapolis Journal*, September 23, 1923. The fact that this was said in the last report of Boeckmann's stay on earth indicates that his image must have been accepted, perhaps with some affectionate humor, by the community. And, indeed, it should have been, especially by the Norwegian immigrant community, because Boeckmann did not only look his role but carried it out.

Boeckmann gave the community the images that established its identity and made it proud: famous Norwegians, such as Ibsen, Bjornson, and Grieg; famous immigrants, such as Knute Nelson, Colonel Hans Heg, and the religious leader Elling Eielsen; favorite Norwegian types, such as the sea pilot; and quite commonly, the good life in America. While Boeckmann was the consummate immigrant artist, he also related to the American community through painting its great men, such as Governor (later President) William McKinley and Lincoln; its great battles, such as the politically incorrect one of the Eighth Minnesota Volunteers with the Sioux at Kildeer Mountain, North Dakota; and local people of prominence like Governor J.S. Pillsbury, Cyrus Northrop, and T.B. Walker. It was indeed Walker who gave Boeckmann his most important link with the American community by hiring him as a restorer of works in his private collection.

The major primary source on Boeckmann's background is what he told a reporter from *Vikværingen*, a publication of immigrants from Kristiania (now Oslo), for an article published January 17, 1917. He was born January 29, 1867, in Kristiania and began studying art at Knud Bergslien's school in 1883. Two years later he got instruction from Norway's great early naturalist Christian Krohg (1852–1925) and people in his circle. These included the internationally best known Norwegian painter at the time, Frits Thaulow (1847–1906), on whose yacht Boeckmann was when he made a sketch of Oslofjord which was the basis for a painting he presented to Kristianialaget, the organization behind *Vikværinger* that was publishing the article. This all reads like a fairy tale, especially considering that the boy was only 18. The names mentioned in Krohg's circle and on Thaulow's yacht are right for the time so Boeckmann most likely was speaking from memory rather than imagination. Just how much he actually studied with these people is another matter.

He left Norway at nineteen and roamed America for twenty years before showing up in the Minneapolis City Directory in 1907, remaining here until his death September 21, 1923. He may have been here earlier, but in 1905 when he married Marie Finstad, a Norwegian from Eidsvold, he was in Milwaukee.

What legacy did Boeckmann leave beyond that referred to? Having wandered for almost 20 years since his very early education, he arrived as something of a highly precocious primitive, but this does not diminish his significance. It is precisely what gives Boeckmann's work interest. He dared to take on anything. Minnesota had few, if any, painters in 1915 who would have attempted the Chickamauga painting (Ill. 38). Boeckmann just went at it, graphed out his battle and lined up the soldiers in proper position one after the other into the distance. He knew what had to be there, and he painted it. The result is a convincing presentation of a highly complex subject, especially fine in the relationship of human activity to the landscape.

The same kind of daring is shown in the painting of his family reading the *Minneapolis Journal*. It is no easy task to paint a group portrait in a rather expansive interior like this one. Boeckmann again simply gives us a well-drawn interior and lines up the three family members in natural poses across it. The composition is held together more by rhythmic horizontal lines than by a unifying space. In the pilot head illustrated here (Ill. 3), Boeckmann made a refreshing departure from the tight and linear style, found especially in the portraits, and gives us indeed some of the airiness and lively brush strokes of Thaulow. The painting is an anomaly of the kind that keeps Boeckmann interesting and gives him a special place in painting by Minnesotans of Norwegian background.

EINAR DAHL 1884–1976
Illustrations 27, 51

In spite of his dedication to art, Einar Dahl never allowed himself to become dependent on it for a living. It was always free expression without commercial considerations. He said in an interview, "I thought once of making a living of it, but...to heck with that noise."

Born the son of a shoemaker Martinus Evenson April 4, 1884, on Hansaasen, Ringsaker, Hedemark, he was the consummate craftsman. For several years immediately after immigration in 1902 at age eighteen, he refined his leather skills in harness shops in Lennox and Fairfax, South Dakota. By 1907 Dahl was in Minneapolis working as a harness maker, and as a salesman, including at Dayton's and Donaldson's. In 1930 he was at the Northwest Artificial Limb Company, Minneapolis. The making of artificial limbs became his major but not his exclusive occupation until his retirement in the mid 1950s.

Art had been in the picture since Einar was a school boy and saw an illustration in his textbook of the Norwegian painter Hans Dahl (1849–1937) at work. The similarity in names sparked the thought of his too becoming a painter. The first real Hans Dahl he saw was in the public library in Minneapolis, where J.B. Walker was exhibiting his *Crossing the Fjord*. He did not seriously start painting until 1910 when he married a Swedish-Minnesotan who he said brought enough stability in his life for this to happen. When it did, none of the sweet romanticism of his original mentor shows up in his work. He never had formal training in art but is said to have received some counsel from the local painters Knute Heldner (1877–1952), Otto Moilan, and Carl O. Erickson (b. 1891).

After Dahl had a work accepted at the 1923 annual exhibition sponsored by the Norwegian Club in Chicago, where he exibited again in 1924 and 26, he became a regular participant in local exhibitions. These included the annual State Fair exhibitions in 1927, 32–33, 39–43, 50, and 55, and he received a first prize there in 1941 on his print *Factory Entrance*. They also included the annual exhibitions for local artists at the Minneapolis Institute of Arts in 1933, 35, 39, 41, and 45. He participated by invitation in the Minnesota Territorial Centennial Fine Arts Exhibition in 1949 and The Parade of Minnesota Painters in 1951, both held on the State Fair grounds. The honor that got him most attention was having his painting *Mystic Hollow* (Ill. 27) accepted for showing in the American Art Today Gallery at the New York World's Fair during its second year, 1940.

Mystic Hollow marks a meeting of two directions in Dahl's painting that coexisted from the late 1930s until his death on March 8, 1976. One was essentially realistic and the other abstract. *Mystic Hollow* is a landscape that is formalized by reducing it to clearly defined planes of somewhat arbitrarily chosen colors. These, Dahl said, were inspired by the coloration on a certain species of duck. It all came together, according to the artist, in a dream after he had been struggling with how to capture a view he had seen near Mazeppa in southeastern Minnesota. This abstracting of a realistic subject is somewhat unusual in Dahl's work. Though he structures his realistic paintings well, they are generally quite distinct from his abstractions.

The story of the dream is characteristic for Dahl, who experienced a spiritual world as directly as the material. He looked on his abstractions as products of that other world and as having their own story and meaning apart from subject matter. There is an inexplicable "rightness" about Dahl's best abstractions, of which *Basic Forms* (Ill. 50) is one, that indicate he may actually have linked into some highter source of art, whatever the nature of that might be. He began exhibiting them as early as 1939 when abstraction was all but unknown in Minnesota. The total lack of critical response may have led to his producing comparatively few, a great loss to Minnesota art.

In spite of the above, Dahl was no ivory tower artist. He was actively involved in the major art associations of his time and contributed to the founding of the Walker Art Center, on whose board he served for a short time. He felt closely attached to his immediate surroundings and in his late years became something of a regionalist in the Minneapolis suburb of Robbinsdale where he lived.

SYDNEY GLEN FOSSUM 1909–1978
Illustration 39

No artist of Norwegian background in Minnesota was more prolific or got more press than Sydney Fossum. In Kay Spangler's survey of serial art exhibitions in Minnesota and the artists who exhibited at them between 1900 and 1970, 180 works by Syd Fossum are listed, which may be a record. It is at least 35 more than by his prolific Swedish-American contemporary, Dewey Albinson (1898–1971). Ten of Fossum's entries won first award and many second, which may also be a record. He exhibited outside the state as well in places like Chicago, Seattle and Denver, again receiving awards. The number resulted in part from his exhibiting in several categories, for he was equally adept in oils, water colors, drawings, and prints. Some were purchase awards, which make him also better represented than most Minnesota artists in museums. These include the Museum of Modern Art, New York; the Seattle Art Museum; the Newark Museum; and in Minneapolis the Institute of Arts, the Walker, and the Weisman. All this brought media coverage.

But media space came also from Fossum's nature. "During my forty years as an artist," he once said, "I've been at war with something." This was generally the establishment and a money-driven culture. His attacks were with words, and he was an excellent writer, often submitting letters to the editor and articles to newspapers or radical journals. He was sharp, witty, but ultimately balanced and intensely human.

Occasionally Fossum's protests took the form of action, as when he twice defied regulations of the federal art programs, in which he was heavily involved from 1933 to 1943, and was indicted and even imprisoned. The first indictment, relating to an organized revolt, was dropped and the demands satisfied. The second was for accepting payment for work which was submitted but had been done outside the period for which payment was claimed. Officials discovered that during this time he was essentially on vacation in New York. The case came to court but he was acquitted after bringing evidence that what he did was common practice in spite of the rules. There was something of a game in this, and the media loved it, taking his side.

One must ask where someone so gifted and yet controversial came from. He was born in Aberdeen, South Dakota, on November 18, 1909, to George F. Fossum, distinguished architect whose father Andrew had come from Christiania (now Oslo) in 1868 and practiced as a building contractor in Aberdeen. His mother Olava (Olive) Korsedahl Fossum had come to the area as a child from Stranden near Alesund, Norway. The fact that his father's lineage was urban and in a profession requiring intelligence as well as aesthetic and manual skills sets Fossum apart from the average midwesterner of Norwegian background. His training was at the Minneapolis School of Art and the Art Student League of New York. Syd was in every sense urban. He died in San Francisco on February 23, 1978, but it may be revealing that his ashes were interred in the family lot, Aberdeen, South Dakota.

More than an artist and agitator, Fossum gave generously of himself to a variety of causes. He served as artist for the Minneapolis Civilian Defense Council in 1942 and as an army field artillery man in France and Germany, 1943–45. He was a founder of the Minnesota Artists Union and held high offices in the Minnesota Artists Association and Artists Equity. He taught, first in the federal art programs and then at the Minneapolis School of Art 1945–50, Washington University (Seattle) 1950–55, Des Moines Art Center summers 1953–57, Duluth Art Center 1960–62, and other places.

One would have expected Fossum to retain a greater presence than he has in the local art scene. One problem may be that he did not have a specific signature style. He could be a social realist, an expressionist, a surrealist, or a pure designer. One thing he could not be was totally abstract. To him art and ideas were one, and the human was essential. His awards may have resulted more from the freshness of his work as a highly intelligent man who never lost a boyish quirkiness than from the fundamental artistic qualities in it, although it was these he strove for. When one now looks at *The Meeting* (Ill. 39) with its deep insight into human need, or at his whimsical portraits of his wife Bunny, or at his frighteningly expressionistic portraits of himself, one wonders if Fossum is not due for reevaluation.

HERBJORN GAUSTA 1854–1924
Illustrations 6–10, 42

If a Norwegian American knows the name of any artist at all from his or her background, it is apt to be Gausta. This is partly due to his having painted altars for about 400 Norwegian-American Lutheran churches; to his paintings having appeared in framable reproductions in the popular church publication *Jul i Vesterheimen* (Christmas in our western home); to his having been given attention in *Telesoga*, a publication of his provincial society; and his having been the first artist of Norwegian background to be researched and published (See Marion Nelson in "Sources").

When I wrote the monograph on Gausta thirty years ago, I referred to him as the first professional artist of Norwegian background active in America. That no longer proves to be true. The research of Katherine M. Littell has brought to light the Oslo-born Chris Jorgensen (1860–1935) who, while six years younger than Gausta, was Assistant Director at The California School of Design, San Francisco, from 1881 to 1884 when Gausta was just returning from his studies in Munich and attempting to get established. My own research brought to light John Hammerstad (1842–1925) who had established himself as a professional artist in Chicago already in 1869. The most recent discoveries were that the illusive Peter Lund was exhibiting in Minneapolis in 1883 and Charles Thoresen in 1886, five and two years respectively before Gausta settled here.

In spite of not being the first, Gausta was at the turn of the century the artist of Norwegian background most closely linked with the immigrant community while also having a place in the local American art scene. He was born in Vestfjorddalen, Tinn, Telemark on June 16, 1854, and came at age 13 with his parents to a small farm near Harmony in southeastern Minnesota. Five years later he entered a three-year program at nearby Luther College in Decorah, Iowa, which he completed in 1875. Later that year he sailed for Kristiania (now Oslo) with financial assistance from Norwegian Americans of prominence in Harmony and Decorah to study art, an unusually early example of immigrant community support of a cultural endeavor. He entered Knud Bergslien's art school, but three years later left for Munich, Germany, to enter the Academy of Art, a mecca for both Norwegian and American students at the time.

On receiving his diploma in 1881, he visited his family in Telemark and returned home. The next five years found him in Chicago, Madison and La Crosse, Wisconsin, and again in Decorah. By the late summer of 1887, he was back on the farm of his mother's family, Gardjord in Rauland, Telemark, where he had earlier developed his interest in landscape and from which much of his Norwegian subject matter, including *Young Mother* (Ill. 7) and *Summertime* (Ill. 8), was drawn. Fall found him again in Munich, winter on the Isle of Capri in Italy, and summer once again in Rauland. Late in 1888 he settled in Minneapolis with a studio in the Tribune Tower. This city would remain his home and the landscape around Harmony, Willmar, and Akeley his major new source of subject matter until he died May 22, 1924.

The move turned out to be a complete break in Gausta's life because within a year of making it the Tribune Tower burned with everything that Gausta owned, including over 100 oils by him and his student friends and innumerable sketches and photographs intended for painting. This shock may have had much to do with the laid-back attitude that many have considered typical of Gausta's later years, something that I once credited to the lack of artistic stimulation. The stimulation was here in people like Alexis Fournier (1865–1945) and Alex Grinager, but Gausta was no longer the pusher who got himself from a small farm in southeast Minnesota to the Academy in Munich and a medal there as best student in the class.

My research since the 1960s indicates that while not aggressive, Gausta was more active in the Minnesota art scene than has generally been realized. He was included in the Minneapolis Industrial Exposition Art Exhibitions in 1890, 91, and 93; in the loan exhibition of the Minneapolis Society of Fine Arts, 1897, and that society's annual exhibitions 1900, 01, 02, and 04; in the small and exclusive Minneapolis Art League 1897 (on the jury and illustrated in the catalogue), and its successor The Artists League of Minneapolis 1908, 10 (two exhibitions) and 15; in the Minnesota State Arts Annual Exhibition 1904, 05, and 10; the annual exhibitions of the work of Minneapolis artists 1916 and 17; and a select exhibition of Minneapolis art shown in Fargo, North Dakota, 1907.

ALEXANDER GRINAGER 1865–1949
Illustrations 36, 44

The roots of Grinager, as of many of our artists, are not so much in Norway as in an established Norwegian-American culture. Born in Albert Lea, Minnesota, January 26, 1865, Alex was the son of Mons Grinager, who emigrated in 1853 from a large and prosperous farm in Brandbu, Hadeland, Norway, and gained Civil War fame as a captain in Col. Heg's 15th Wisconsin Regiment. He was wounded but returned to Albert Lea where he was active in politics until he moved to Minneapolis where he is listed in the city directory of 1885–86 as a cashier at the Scandia Bank, of which he would become vice president. Alex was twenty at the time of the move and had already been in the city studying under the Danish-American decorator Peter Clausen (1830–1924) and the Philadelphia landscapist C. W. Knapp (1823–1900) who must have been visiting in the area.

Alex's parents Mons and Anna Egge Grinager took the boy back to Europe to enter him in an art school, an impressive example of parental support of an artist. The U.S. Minister to Denmark, Rasmus B. Anderson, with whom Mons may have had connections since both were in their time vice presidents of Scandia Bank, persuaded Alex to enroll in the Royal Academy of Art in Copenhagen. There he studied for three years with the best of the Danish academicians, Carl Bloch (1834–1890), Johan Fr. Vermehren (1823–1910), and Otto Bache (1839–1927), going north in the summers to sketch in Norway and Sweden. Being an accomplished violinist, he made the acquaintance of the composers Edvard Grieg and Christian Sinding, whom he painted on a walking tour of the mountains. Alex continued to study at the Julien Academy in Paris under Paul Laurens (1870–1934) and J.J. Benjamin Constant (1842–1902) but appears to have gained most from his 1893 exposure to Monet and travel to Italy.

Grinager's Norwegian background is clear, but his being a Minnesotan is less so. His listing in the Minneapolis Directory ends in 1896 and he remains in New York and its environs until his death in Ossining on March 8, 1949. He had, however, established himself in the local art scene by exhibiting four works at the Minneapolis Industrial Exposition of 1891 and thirteen at the same exposition two years later. He participated in both the first two exhibitions of the Minneapolis Art League during the year of his departure and again in its May, 1897, exhibition. When that was replaced by the Artists League of Minneapolis, he exhibited with it from 1910 to 1915. That year he also participated in the St. Paul Art Institute's First Annual Exhibition of Northwestern Artists, indicating that he must still have considered himself a Minnesotan. In 1910 he had also been given a one-man exhibition of twelve works at the Odin Club of Minneapolis.

In New York Grinager exhibited extensively at the Salmagundi Club and with Allied Artists of America at the New York Historical Society from 1911 until two years before his death. He was also shown in Paris, where reviews stressed the Norwegian character of his work, and for three years, 1919–21, in England, in both London and St. Ives. He was the most international of early Minnesota artists with Norwegian background.

Grinager's major reputation was gained as a painter of murals and stage designs, most, if not all, of which are gone. For architects McKim, Mead, and White he covered all the walls of one floor in the Grand Central Palace with *Streets of Bagdad*. In 1916 he painted *Panorama of the History of the U.S. Navy* for the San Francisco World's Fair, a U.S. government commission; and, again as a government commission in 1932, he did six murals for the Century of Progress Exposition, Chicago. But his reputation may have been gained as much from his design and execution of stage effects for David Belasco, including his productions of *Ben Hur* and *Chanticleer*. He also served at various times as chief designer and artist for the companies of Ernest Albert, Castle and Harvey; Gates and Morange; and Lee, Lash and Miller.

As an easel painter Grinager covered a variety of subjects, but in style he retained the semi-impressionistic, light-filled quality of *Venice* (Ill. 36) and *Boys Bathing* (Ill. 44). He mentions the importance of Monet in his development but also of Danish Naturalists such as Peder Severin Krøyer (1851–1909). His conservative approach to Impressionism comes close to theirs. Landscapes, often with water, and street scenes are prominent in his work, but he is also a competent figure painter as revealed specifically by the sitting boy on the right in *Boys Bathing*.

SVERRE HANSSEN 1891–1968
Illustration 32

Only one easel painting by Sverre Hanssen is known to have been on public display in Minnesota during his lifetime. *Fishing boats off Norwegian Coast* was shown at the Norse-American Centennial Art Exhibition in St. Paul in 1925, the year after his arrival to that city from Norway. After his death in February 1968 in Seattle, where he had moved from Minneapolis four years earlier, numerous oils were discovered in his estate. His first one-man exhibition was held posthumously at the American-Swedish Institute in Minneapolis during May and June, 1968. The thirty works in it and his *Train Yards* (Ill. 32), which was painted as a WPA art project about 1940, reveal Hanssen's ability as a precise imitator of nature and a sensitive colorist. The meticulous draftsmanship and carefully calculated perspective in works like *Train Yards* strike one first; but in spite of their precision they acquire atmosphere and lightness through the use of color. His subject matter is largely serene: boats in harbor, spring in the Rockies, swans, women and children. The seascapes can, on the other hand, acquire an almost disturbing inner intensity, undoubtedly reflecting Hanssen's intimate experience with the subject as a young fisherman.

Hanssen made no reference in material that has come to light as to why he did not exhibit, but it may have been because he was as a European-trained decorator a pure academic realist (with a bit of romantic expressionism in his seascapes) and felt that he could not compete with artists working in more contemporary modes. In actuality he would have held up well if for no other reason than the sheer perfection of his product. He could have given needed breadth to the Twin Cities' art scene in the generation before Richard Lack (b. 1928) made his entry.

Hanssen did not consider himself a born artist. He says a major reason for his becoming one was that his brothers and sisters laughed at his clumsy drawings when as kids they were put around a table with pencils and tablets to be quiet when their father, a schoolteacher, took his traditional nap after dinner. Sverre set out to silence that laughter. This all happened in Austnesfjord on the remote fishing islands of Lofoten where Sverre was born in 1891. His task was not easy.

When Sverre was still a small boy, his father died and he was farmed out to an uncle on Hadseløya in Vesterålen, where he became a fisherman for the fishing magnate Kristian Fredriksen, whom he despised as a capitalist but who ultimately supported him as an artist.

Sverre had continued to work on his goal. He hired out to an established Swedish artist Richard Lindström (1882–1943) who needed an assistant when he came to paint the rugged north Norwegian landscape in the summer, and he was ultimately willing to assist the boy in his art. This led to Sverre at age 23 becoming an apprentice to the decorator Gunnar Larsen in Svolvær. When he returned to his uncle and Fredriksen, he was an accomplished painter and was asked to decorate the improvised hall where King Haakon V was to be entertained in connection with the opening of a new sea passage that linked Risøysundet with Andfjorden. Coffee was served in Kristian Fredriksen's garden, and the host arranged for his old fisherman to have a conversation with His Majesty. Shortly after, Sverre, his wife, and one son left for St. Paul.

Sverre was immediately employed by St. Paul decorating companies and also got commissions as a freelancer. When decorator work was limited, he painted houses. Although a professed agnostic, he was involved in the decoration of about 75 churches in Minnesota, North Dakota, Iowa, and Wisconsin, and was much liked by Catholic priests. Father Louis Gales even gave him a room for a period in the James J. Hill house, the location of the exhibition to which this publication relates, when it was being used by the Catechetical Guild. Catholic churches in St. Paul alone where he worked include Assumption, St. Agnes, and St. Casimer. There he also worked in Gloria Dei Lutheran. But the building with which he is most closely associated is the Minnesota State Capitol, where he did restoration and new decoration over a period of ten years, including applying gold leaf to the dome and the horses over the entry.

Hanssen is linked to the literary scene in Minneapolis through being the grandfather of Erik Utne of Utne Magazine and through marrying in his late sixties the writer Brenda Ueland, whose family had also been among the few Norwegian-American art patrons in the state.

LLOYD HERFINDAHL 1922–1996
Illustrations 21–22

Herfindahl was born in Emmons, Minnesota, near Albert Lea, June 15, 1922, to Albert Herfindahl and to Ingeborg (Betsy) Singelstad Herfindahl. She had roots in the Bergen area, and Lloyd liked to think of himself as a "Bergenser." He felt close to his Norwegian background in spite of considering Paris a second home.

Herfindahl was one of the most complex and gifted artists in the state at his time, but he was never completely accepted by the local art establishment. There were several problems. Like Berge and Boeckmann, he remained outside the local art organizations and did not participate in the annual exhibitions. More serious might have been his tendency in later years to make much of links with prestigious-sounding but obscure European institutions and with people of stature, who he managed whenever possible to be photographed with. This did not sit well with the art world in Minneapolis. Because of it, his art was not given the attention it deserved in his lifetime, which came to an end January 21, 1996. By then he was a loner on the local art scene, but his community in Albert Lea gave support and showed appreciation.

Two difficulties exist in evaluating Herfindahl. One is the extreme breadth of his work both in type and in quality, and the other an unusual way of looking at art and the world that makes him a man apart. To begin with the latter, he sees the moment of a painting as also representing time. In *History of Norway* contemporary figures stand for the greats of the past. The Minister of Culture, Alv Heltne, for example, is Ibsen. They do not take on the image of those they represent because, as products of the past, they are that past. He looked on his art in the same way. If someone asked how old one of his paintings was, he would say 4000 years, in other words, the approximate age of the history of painting as we know it.

This telescoping of time also led to his incorporating historical materials relating to a subject into his presentation of it. Swatches of old miners' blankets, for example, were imbedded in his painting of the mining industry in Minnesota. The psychology is the same as that behind relics in religion, making the past one with the present. The painting by this means is no longer "about something," he says, "it *is* that thing."

As to types of work, a major category is murals. In them an attempt is generally made to put history within one large frame, as in *The History of the Judicial System* (Albert Lea Courthouse), *Homage to Agriculture, The Evolution of Farming* (Cenex Corporation Headquarters), *The Bible in History* (Aurora University, Illinois). The literary element in these is disturbing from a strictly aesthetic standpoint, but Herfindahl brings unity into the span of time through coherence in the overall composition. His achievement in this is especially impressive when one considers that his art training was limited, a period of study at the Minneapolis School of Fine Arts with Cameron Booth (1892–1980) and Syd Fossum and some apparently less formal study with Adolf Dehn (1895–1968) and Oskar Kokoschka (1886–1980) elsewhere.

Of smaller works, too, one category, the "multiple image" drawings and prints, involves the telescoping of time. In these, one image a la Salvador Dali (1904–1989) helps construct another. A well-known example is *The Prophecy*, a profile head of Christ in which the hair and beard are made up of shepherds, angels, and Old Testament prophets. Although requiring an unusual vision to create, these do not come across as profound attempts to bring time into a static image.

The best of Herfindahl is found in his more straightforward works, sometimes portraits but more often scenes from country or city life. They can be realistic depictions of society's rejects; they can be caricatures, like *Threshing Time* (Ill. 22), which shows the essential gluttony of a country dinner rather than the external dignity shown by artists like Grant Wood (1892–1941); or they can be penetrating exposures of the isolation in which country women in particular can find themselves trapped, as in *Captive* (Ill. 21).

The above reached the public through exhibitions arranged by the artist in restaurants, banks, or other public places, only occasionally galleries and never serial exhibitions.

ARNOLD N. KLAGSTAD 1898–1954
Illustrations 25, 33

Klagstad is not only of Norwegian background, but the product of a Norwegian-American *art* environment. He was born in Marinette, Wisconsin, July 14, 1898, as the oldest child of the established Norwegian-born painter August Klagstad (see next page) and Othelia Ness Klagstad. He came to Minneapolis with his parents in 1915 and was enrolled in North High School the following year. A stint in the Navy, where he became a radio operator, second class, broke off his formal education. Experience gained in the Navy perhaps led to his taking a year of study at Dunwoody Institute in 1921 in preparation for becoming an electrician.

All along there must have been some involvement in his father's profession because in October 1923 he exhibited *River Bank* in the Ninth Annual Exhibition of Work by Local Artists at the Minneapolis Institute of Arts and lists it at $150, a substantial price at the time. Two years later he enters the Minneapolis School of Fine Arts studying under Morris Davidson (b. 1898) and David Angarola (1893–1929), one of the earliest artists to explore Swede Hollow and the river flats for motifs. *The Flats* is the name of Klagstad's entry in the 1930 Annual Exhibition at the Institute, and the Mississippi has a place, though secondary, in a great many of Klagstad's works.

Key to Klagstad's development was three months spent in 1931 at the Fontainbleau School of Art in France working under Gaston Balande (b. 1881), André Strauss (b. 1885), and Jean Despujols (b. 1886). He joined Despujols again for another three months of study in Paris, where he spent his evenings sketching at the Academy Colarossi. It must have been in France that he refined his sense of form, so characteristic of his later work. Mary Swanson has justifiably related his well-structured cityscapes, which usually include a bit of landscape, to Corot's paintings from his early period in Rome.

On his return to Minneapolis Klagstad accelerated his pattern of exhibiting as his total record of participation in the local exhibitions shows. He was at the State Fair in 1925, 27–28, 30, and 32–40, and in the annual exhibitions of the Minneapolis Institute of Arts in 1923, 25, 29, and 31–39. He appears to be the only artist in our group who exhibited in the annual exhibitions of Twin Cities artists at the St. Paul Gallery and School of Art in 1940–41, the only two years it was in existense. At the State Fair he won the second award in landscape for three consecutive years, 1933, 34, and 35. Although these specific works are not known, they probably had the partial faceting of the various elements that gives *Ilgen Falls* (Ill. 25) from 1940 its clear structure. The sudden break in Klagstad's exhibition record came with his serving in the Navy during World War II and coming back to replace his aging father in the family's church furnishing business.

Although Arnold must have been financially secure as a bachelor who from 1926 to his death in May, 1954, was intermittently involved in the family's business, he qualified for the federally funded art programs of the 1930s and 1940s. When the short-lived PWAP ended in April, 1934, he was one of seven artists in the program given continued employment by the University to record in paint the campus as it was then. In addition to Klagstad, the group included Dewey Albinson (1898–1971), Cameron Booth (1892–1980), Stanford Fenelle (b. 1909), Syd Fossum, Erle Loran (1908–1999), and Elof Wedin (1901–1983), essentially the major Minnesota artists at the time. Klagstad with his love of painting buildings in natural settings was, with the possible exception of Loran, the most qualified for this specific assignment and left ten fine paintings of quiet character and modest size that are now in the Weisman Art Museum.

While active in the late thirties with the Minnesota Artists Association, of which he was a founder, and the Artists Union, Klagstad did not receive awards. In 1940, however, the Metropolitan Museum of Art, New York, purchased his *Industrial Landscape* of 1937, a work resembling *Washington-Crosby Elevator* (Ill. 33), the first purchase this institution made of a work by a Minneapolis artist. Typically, however, this midwestern painting was deaccessioned in 1991 and sold by Sotheby's. Attempts to trace its whereabouts have failed.

Like Boeckmann, Klagstad was an artist who served his community, both the immigrant and the established American. Starting with the first, he is said to have painted at least 1,000 altar pieces (the figure is higher in some sources) for Norwegian-American churches; he was in 1925 a founder of the Modum-Eiker Lag, an organization of immigrants from his home area in Norway; he represented a committee of all these organizations in establishing a relief program for Norway immediately after the German occupation in April, 1940; he belonged to the Sons of Norway; he made two trips to Norway and wrote on both of them in immigrant and American publications.

Klagstad was born on August 14, 1866, at Vingen between Øvre Eiker and Modum in the Drammen area of Norway to Torger and Karen Klagstad. When he was only five, the family emigrated and soon settled in Manistique, Michigan, where Torger got employment in the lumber industry. August too worked at the mill where he accidentally cut his foot. This freed him from work and allowed him to go to school, a story paralleled in that of Olaf Aalbu, Sr., and other artists. The year was 1884, and Klagstad was eighteen. After a look at his education and further developments, we will consider his role in the American community.

Bookkeeping seemed like an appropriate area for the boy as preparation for business, so he entered Valparaiso Normal School and Business Institute in Indiana. There he met an artist whom he engaged for instruction. This got him on the road he would follow until his death March 7, 1949.

From 1884 to 1895, Klagstad is listed in the Chicago city directory as an artist. During this time he did finishing work on photo enlargements. The process was undoubtedly the usual one at the time of embellishing the original with pencil, chalk, and airbrushes, either in black and white or color. In addition to periods of work in Boston and Brooklyn, he took courses at the Chicago Academy of Art. He did not study at the Art Institute of Chicago until 1912 and 1915 when he was already established in his own studio in Marinette, Wisconsin. Both people he studied with at the Institute were known for their portraits, W.J. Reynolds (1866–1930) for his Chicago celebrities, and Elbridge Ayer Burbank (1858–1949) for his Indians. Klagstad's choice is not surprising since in 1912 he began to develop portraiture as a specialty. His work with photographs gave him excellent preparation for this. He already had a reputation for altarpieces after contributing a *Christ in Gethsemane* to his home church in Manistique and getting commissions as a result. This was back in about 1886 when he was on a trip home from Valparaiso. It was probably altar painting that in 1915 led to his settling in Minneapolis, where the headquarters of the largest body of Norwegian Lutherans was located.

Klagstad's link with the American community came largely through his portraits. He also did them for the immigrant community but did not, like Boeckmann, paint Norway's great men. He did, on the other hand, in 1923 make an impressive copy of Thomas Sully's full-length portrait of George Washington; and, as the most professional portrait painter in the area, he was commissioned to do such local greats as the founder of the Great Northern Railway, James J. Hill, and of the First National Bank of St. Paul, Parker Paine. Both are from photographs, as were most if not all his portraits, and they retain some of the character of the highlighted pictures that got him into the business. Jamie Besso found that they became freer and more relaxed as time went on.

A middle life change in Klagstad's style is marked in his watercolors and unofficial easel paintings as well. He entered the Minnesota State Art Society exhibitions (later State Fair) in 1915–16, 25–26, and 31; and the Minneapolis Institute of Arts exhibitions in 1915, 17, 23, 25–28, and 30. He also exhibited at the first St. Paul Institute of Art exhibition in 1915. His only award was an Honorable Mention at the Minneapolis Institute of Arts in 1915, the first year he was here. About one-third of the entries were portraits, but not of an official nature. The early landscapes and still lifes are tightly painted, but a broad and more structural style develops during the mid twenties. A watercolor of a falls from a 1930s trip to Norway has much of the same character as his son's *Ilgen Falls* (Ill. 25) from 1940. Cross influences appear strong at this time. The father's impressive *Still Life* (Ill. 50) shown here, apparently the one exhibited at the State Fair in 1931, has a boldness of execution and clarity of form that sets it completely apart from his commissioned work.

ANDREAS R. LARSEN 1877–1942
Illustration 40

The name Andreas Larsen has been lost completely from public memory, but his work is perhaps seen and appreciated more than that of most Minnesota painters of Norwegian background. Larsen designed and produced stained glass that is in many churches and some secular buildings throughout the upper midwest; precisely which ones is difficult to determine. The names of artist-craftsmen did not remain with their products like those of fine artists. Larsen may have been totally forgotten if the Athenaeum of Minneapolis had not purchased several boxes of studies shortly after his death late in 1942. These are now in Special Collections at the Minneapolis Public Library.

Investigation indicates that Larsen was far from being an unknown in his time. He was born on Rud in Veldre, Hedemark, in 1877. He took training as an interior decorator but gave it up for a time to try his hand at business. Painting was his great love, and it was in this area that he got a scholarship for study in Europe. He spent his time in Nuremberg learning the fundamentals of drawing and design. He went from Germany to France, and finally in 1903 to New York where he studied for about a year.

Larsen's midwest career began in Chicago where he was an interior decorator for Marshall Field's. A newspaper want-ad from the Minneapolis glass and paint firm Forman, Ford, and Company led to his becoming head of its art glass department and moving permanently to Minneapolis in 1909. He remained with that firm until founding his own Stained and Leaded Glass Company with Edward Gertsch about 1923. It was located on Hennepin Avenue near Lake, where it remained until his death.

Larsen did not have glass experience when he came. He was an artist, which is evident from his extensive exhibition record from 1911 to 1921. He had generally two or more works, usually oils, in the following juried annual exhibitions: Artists League of Minneapolis, 1911–13; a special show of Attic Club members at the Minneapolis Society of Fine Arts, 1913; Attic Club exhibitions, 1913 (at State Fair) and 16 (at Beard Gallery); Annual Exhibition of Minneapolis Artists, 1915–16, 21; and the Norse-American Centennial Fine Arts Exhibition (St. Paul), 1925. At the Attic Club exhibition in 1913 he got a second award in oils and a third in water colors. At the Norse-American Centennial Exhibition, which was national, he got a second in watercolors. None of the works listed in these exhibitions or any of their type has come to light. Most exhibiting stops around the time he established his own business in 1923.

Larsen was an active member of the Minneapolis art community, being a founding member of its first organization of professional artists initiated in 1910 by the assistant director of the Minneapolis School of Fine Arts Theodore J. Keane of San Francisco. His name is the only one that sounds Scandinavian on the list of founders but many, including Magnus Norstad and Arnold Klagstad, later joined through having their work approved by a committee.

Judging from his commercial work, Larsen was an artist of exceptional talent. His stained glass window style was essentially Medieval, but he could create with great freedom within it. Occasionally his figures, as in *Resurrection* (Ill. 40), can have an Art Nouveau character in line as well as color. He did not design the large scenes of Louis Tiffany (1848–1943) or John LaFarge (1835–1910) but constructed his windows of small sections of colored glass, with red and blue dominating in those of traditional character. The effect is jewel-like and has great brilliance. Norway had been early in the return to this approach but since Larsen was not in glass there and left before the new style gained prominence, he may have learned it here. He was a friend of and much admired by the greatest of American stained glass artists at the time, Charles J. Connick (1875–1945) of Boston.

Some of the watercolor studies by Larsen in Special Collections, Minneapolis Public Library, have the names of local churches where his works might exist: St. Louis Park Congregational; Gustavus Adolphus, Northeast; Hamline University Methodist; Hopkins German Lutheran; Christ Church, St. Paul; Swedish Tabernacle, Minneapolis; Arlington Hills Lutheran, St. Paul; and Richfield Lutheran at Wentworth and 58th Street, Minneapolis. The reason for uncertainty is that the studies in some cases may simply be proposals which were never carried out.

PETER F. LUND (dates unknown)
Illustrations 1–2

Lund has for years been a mystery in Minnesota painting. No vital statistics that can be definitely associated with him have come to light. There is not even documentation of his being Norwegian although both Rena Cohn *(Painting and Sculpture in Minnesota, 1820–1914)* and Mary Swanson *(The Divided Heart)* have considered him so.

Lund is being presented as Norwegian in this study as well purely because the Norwegian Art Society in Minneapolis showed two of his works at the Second Minneapolis Industrial Exposition in 1887. There are two disturbing indications that he might have been a Dane. One is that the title *Sea View on the Coast of Denmark* is given for one of the paintings at the Exposition, and the other is that Lee Rokke found a Peter Lund from Denmark in Hennepin County who when applying for citizenship gave his date of arrival in the United States as June 7, 1883, the first year that our Lund is listed in the *Minneapolis City Directory*. One thing speaks against their being the same person. Our Lund exhibited in the First Loan Exhibition sponsored by the Minneapolis Society of Fine Arts that very year. If he arrived in June he would have had to do quick work making himself known as an artist here.

Whatever Lund's background, he established himself as a professional artist in Minneapolis very rapidly, having a studio downtown from the beginning and a residence further south, usually in the Lake Calhoun area. From 1890 he also had a studio in Duluth, where he moved his residence as well in 1893. All this speaks of independent wealth or of success, as does his supposed move east about 1897, the year he had a painting in the fall exhibition at the National Academy of Design in New York. It has been accepted by everyone who has written on Lund that he died in 1902, probably because an unidentified typewritten note in the Northeast Regional Historical Library at the University of Minnesota, Duluth has him dying that year, giving a specific address in Boston. No death record in Boston came to light in Rokke's intensive research, but reference did show up to an obituary in the 1898 volume of *Art for America*, VIII, No. 1. This issue has not yet been located. When it is, both Lund's death date and possibly his assumed place of origin could prove wrong.

Lund did not appear only in the two exhibitions mentioned but in the First Minneapolis Industrial Exposition of 1886 as well. His *Storm on the Coast* at that exhibit was illustrated in the catalogue with the comment, "One of a class of pictures in which the artist excels. This is a picture of more than average merit. Mr. Lund is a local artist whose best work should be better known."

As the comment suggests, Lund was primarily a marine painter. Of the examples shown here *Shipwreck* (Ill. 1) is the most typical because of its dramatic content, the consequences of a storm at sea. The drama, however, is usually in the storm itself, often shown at night. *Sailboat off Lighthouse* (Ill. 2) is atypical in having the ship and its grandeur as the central point of interest. In this sense it relates to a little known category of Lund's production, ship portraits. Two examples have appeared on the market, one of the renowned Civil War *Monitor* and the other of the *Christopher Columbus,* a sleek passenger ship painted in 1891. There is a sophistication in these, and definitely in the handling of light and composition in *Sailboat* that indicates Lund had training, at least as a marine painter. If he did not, he must have come to Minnesota with considerable experience in his field. His painting technique is unusual, having none of the tight linearity of the primitive but rather a daubed quality that gives vibrance to the surface. This is especially evident in *Shipwreck*.

Lund's marine scenes are not all generic, nor did he limit himself to them. Two Lunds owned by the Minneapolis Institute of Arts refer to Lake Superior in the titles and are very characteristic of its shoreline. Non-marine subjects, such as *Logging Camp in the Winter* at the St. Louis County Historical Society, Duluth, has a primitive character, but a hunting scene in the same institution reveals considerable sophistication even in the handling of figures. A Lund has recently come to light of a logged-over hill with an industrial smokestack rising in the distance. It suggests that already in the early 1890s he lamented the inroads of industry on that untamed nature so central in his seascapes.

JOHN MAAKESTAD b. 1928
Illustration 28

There are about twelve artists represented here who are not so much of Norwegian as of Norwegian-American background. Two come out of a cultural elite within that background which was closely linked with the Norwegian-American Lutheran Church. One is Cyrus Running and the other John Maakestad. John was born December 12, 1928 in Whitehall, Wisconsin, to Pastor Norvald Maakestad who was in turn the son of a pastor, John Maakestad, well-known for founding congregations in Michigan and elsewhere on the frontier. The elder John was born in Sørfjord, Hardanger, but emigrated at such a young age that even he was educated in an immigrant institution, Luther College, Decorah, Iowa.

The artist's mother, Agnes Linnevold from Decorah, represented a meeting of many families also established in the immigrant elite, Ylvisaker, Jordahl, Jacobson (descendants of Abraham), Sivesind and others. John too, of course, would get his B.A. from a Norwegian-American Lutheran college, St. Olaf, where his mentor as an art and English major was the pastor/art professor Arnold Flaten. One must remember that this Norwegian-American elite, of which John is so totally a product, is a broadly cultural elite in spite of its close relation to the church. In the early Norwegian-American community as in medieval Europe, book learning was found largely among the clergy.

How does this background relate to John, who after a stint in the army that got him acquainted with the art faculty at the University of Indiana and after receiving an MFA from the University of Iowa, joined and eventually replaced his mentor on the staff of St. Olaf College? For one thing, this background was strong and satisfying enough to draw him back into it. This turning in on himself, so to speak, and circumscribing his sphere of operations may seem limiting, but it has, on the other hand, also given him confidence in who he is and courage to develop on that without being intimidated by what is outside. He not only knows who he is but what he wants. He was in the annual exhibitions only six times, all before 1963. An audience or critiques are not important to him because his pursuit is an inner one.

Judging from the art known to me, Maakestad's goal is to capture the energy of nature in line and color. When asked how nature enters into his work he said, "It all comes in one way or another from nature." Originally he included visual reminders of nature in his creations so the viewer would more easily know what the work was about. We see this in *Spring Landscape* (Ill. 28) of 1956, where the subtle transitions of color and shifts from light to dark suggest a specific terrain below an obvious horizon but where in the lower left the colors and patterns begin speaking for themselves, conveying the inner vibrance behind the countryside as it again comes to life. The vehicle, according to the artist, is actually a farm in a very real view from the rural home where he and his family have lived for 45 years. This, like Cezanne's home at Aix-en-Provence, is the fixed point which serves as a control for Maakestad's experiments in catching the dynamics behind nature.

In the next phase of Maakestad's work, the visual clues of what was presented become increasingly integrated with the abstract portrayal of the energy behind it. The color woodcuts of the Norwegian artist Nikolai Astrup (1880–1928) come to mind, but Maakestad says, however, that he does not feel he relates to Norwegian art directly. His attraction is rather to the entire north European tradition with its expressionistic tendencies.

By the seventies the visual clues get all but lost. One is confronted directly with the forces behind nature, in other words, with the source of all life. Maakestad considers himself a pantheist, and here is pantheism carried to the ultimate. But like many artists who arrive at abstraction through internal development, Maakestad retracted from it shortly after he got there. In the early nineties when struggling with lyme disease that was affecting his eyesight, and facing retirement at age 66, he returned to the image. In his broadly painted watercolor landscapes from the early years of the decade, the white of the paper becomes the energizing element, bringing the late Emil Molde to mind. But Maakestad has not stopped there; he is now creating computer-generated abstractions in which the forces behind nature are again being given the form of pure color and line.

HAAKON MELVOLD 1841–1888
Illustrations 4–5

Melvold spent only his last four years in Minnesota, dying in Minneapolis from a stomach ailment, possibly related to malnutrition, at age 46 in 1888. During those four years he was the best trained and most skilled landscape artist in the area, but he left little mark partly because the community was not ready for him and partly because he did not, as far as is known, paint one local subject that could give him a place among the visual chroniclers of the area. All his works appear to be from sketches made in Norway.

Melvold appears to have been exhibited here only three times, all at the Minneapolis Industrial expositions and all through the efforts of the Norwegian Art Society, organized in 1887. Because of the rarity of the catalogues, I will give the listings. The following Melvolds appeared at the exposition of 1887 under "Minneapolis Norwegian Art Society's Collection:" *Waterfall in Gudbrandsdalen, Norway* ($500); *From Tyrifjord Lake* ($500); *Scene in Romsdalen, Norway* ($350); *In the Woods, Østerdalen, Norway* ($350); *From Sognefjord, Norway*; *From Trysil Highlands, Norway*; *Sunset in Norway*; *Hardangerfjord, Norway*; *Rain: Motive* (sic) *from Norway*; *Mjøsen Lake, Norway*; *Norwegian Farm*; *Valdres, Norway*. The exhibit arranged by the Society at the exposition of 1888, the year of Melvold's death, included his *Sunset* (owned by George A. Bracket); *Landscape from Sogn, Norway* ($250); *Waterfall in Norway* ($200); and a collection of sketches that appear to be owned by the Society. At the exposition of 1893, the Norwegian group exhibited the following Melvolds: *Study from Nature, At the Mountain Lake, Waterfall*, and three works entitled *Sketch*.

Purchasers for Melvold paintings were few. The only ones of which there is record are George Bracket, Lars Rand, the banker A.C. Haugen (president of the Norwegian Art Society), and Judge Andreas Ueland. By 1925 he must have been essentially forgotten because there was no special exhibition of his work as there was of work by Herbjorn Gausta, who had died the previous year. The only Melvold was in the Loan Exhibition, *Norwegian Lake*, lent by Judge Ueland. The artist is listed as Harold rather than Haakon.

Born in Rena, Åmodt near Hamar, Norway, September, 1841, Melvold at nineteen was in contact with the art teacher in Christiania (now Oslo) Johan Fredrik Eckersberg (1822–1870), entering his drawing school the following year and his school of painting in 1862. In 1863 he began a four-year period of study on a free tuition scholarship and is known to have contributed a painting to a lottery at Kunstforeningen (The Art Society) in 1869. The next year finds him in Chicago, possibly together with a fellow student from Eckersberg's School, John Hammerstad (1842–1925), who was one of the most prolific painters in Chicago for the next fifty years. It must have been here that Melvold painted his sensitive and melancholy *Rena River* (Ill. 4) in 1871. After the great fire that year, he returned to Norway and from 1876 was an art teacher at the high school in Hamar. He resigned his position in 1884 over a dispute with his siblings and left for America with his wife and four children, this time settling in Minneapolis.

Melvold had been highly regarded by his master Eckersberg, who said "that his good grasp of nature, the substance in his compositions, and his fine sense of mood and color are clear evidence of great talent." He was also highly spoken of as a teacher, but these qualifications were apparently not satisfactory for his success in America. Eckersberg was the least dramatic and most objective of the Norwegian romantics trained in Dusseldorf, Germany. It was this reserve and detailed depiction of nature that left the greatest mark on his student.

Albert Bierstadt had been given a major showing at the First Minneapolis Industrial Exhibition in 1886. He caught the excitement and grandeur of the frontier, and this kind of hype was an element in pioneer life itself. Melvold's reflective, low key works, in spite of the perfection of their execution, could not quite cut it. Even as grand in scale and powerful in composition as his *Waterfalls* (Ill. 5) is, it must be looked at so closely that the detail in the rocks, the moss, and even the gushing water can be seen to appreciate it fully. The landscape is down-scaled rather than overblown, as one sees in the low distant mountain. Realism was reaching both Norway and America by the eighties, and Melvold was already applying some of it in spite of his romantic subject matter.

MARGIT MINDRUM 1899–1975
Illustrations 16–19

Mindrum's background is more immigrant than strictly Norwegian although her father Tarkjel Landsverk (1857–1948) was 25 before he emigrated only fifteen years before Margit, his first child, was born in 1899. Both parents had roots in Telemark, where folk traditions in many arts had remained alive since the Middle Ages.

The mother, Helga Oian Landsverk, was born here to a substantial work-oriented family from Hjartdal, only fourteen miles over the mountain from Seljord where the father was born and raised. Though also completely of peasant stock, he had taken three years of teacher training in Kviteseid and could play folk instruments, carve, and write poetry before leaving. He settled on a farm in the Lanesboro, Minnesota, area, but mostly taught Norwegian parochial school and built houses during the first ten years.

The Landsverk home always had a place for finer things. Tarkjel continued to carve and was not only a superb craftsman but an exceptional designer. He allowed his youngest son, Halvor, to pursue art in spite of his importance on the farm. Cement sculpture was Halvor's early interest, but he later became well known as a carver of Norwegian log chairs. The father and son set up a museum of their work at the farm in the 1930s and charged admission for entry.

Margit's early environment, as seen, was far from without art, but as a woman she had to pursue it cautiously. Her mother in particular felt that one artist in the family was enough and that art was not for women. Work with textiles, on the other hand, was, so Margit hooked rugs as her mother did and learned to do stenciling on linens. One of her rugs has an Art Deco design revealing great creativity.

Margit was over fifty when her mother died and obligations to her family lessened enough for her to paint. She progressed by experimentation and found that her favorite medium was a type of gouache sold in little jars at the dime store as Carter's Water Colors. One thinks of Grandma Moses but the analogy does not quite fit. Nostalgia was not as central for Mindrum, and she moved quickly toward her own academic realism. Her only guidance came from brother Halvor who had taken a correspondence course in art that gave him at least the basics of representation. Her first subjects in the 1950s were the farm with the children playing or coming home from school, the family church, and the like. They may not have been completely current but were not only fond memories from childhood as is often true of older self-taught artists.

By the late 1950s, Mindrum had become primarily a landscapist. Many of the scenes appear to be from Houston county where she lived most of her married life. Some are site-specific, and the more generic works have the character of the local landscape. Painting the four seasons, with a little preference for summer, gave variety to her work (Ill. 16-19). "All," she said, "have their pleasure. Spring comes with Easter, warmth and new life . . . Summer, flowers, berries, and family reunions." Fall brings brilliant colors, "gathering vegetables, nuts, etc." Winter's joy is a different one, it "seems like a dream. My painting project makes it pass by quickly. . . . I completely forget time and space when blending colors . . ." Her mention of Easter relates to the close connection she felt between nature and her Christian faith. Many of her lush meadows with sheep had the inscription "The Lord is my shepherd."

Mindrum worked like a professional, and considering the 600 paintings she completed in her 25-year career, she was one. Not long after filling 57 orders for paintings of one church, all individualized and in the season requested, she wrote that the living room looked "more like a workshop than anything else. Paint jars, brushes, easel, and pictures sitting all around." She kept a record of every painting. Every one was at least a little different from the next. She used models, but she did not follow them or repeat herself exactly. She disliked being brought photographs to copy. She said she was afraid the customer would be disappointed, but the truth may have been that she found it too restricting. When one such customer remarked that she had omitted a bridge, her response was, "If you want the bridge, look at the photograph."

MAGNUS NORSTAD 1884–1962
Illustration 31 and page 66

One of the great mysteries in Minnesota painting has been Magnus Norstad. He is known largely through one painting, *City on a Hill* (Ill. 31), which in 1917 won the Silver Medal Award in the Third Annual Exhibition of Northwestern Artists at the St. Paul Institute. A letter to the editor of the *Pioneer Press* says it "should appeal to the hearts of all natives of this Northwest since it portrays the severity of its icy winter climate only in a mysteriously soft and benignant aspect." The painting came ultimately to the Minnesota Historical Society, where it has appealed to the natives and been considered by authorities a major example of Minnesota art.

My recent research has dispersed the mystery of the artist but not of the painting. Norstad was born June 24, 1884, in Bodø far north in Norway. In an exhibition catalogue statement he says his early fascination with art was so great that he made paint brushes from his own hair. Just before 1900 when not yet fifteen, he came with his parents to Seattle but headed east in 1905 for two years of study at the National Academy of Design in New York. There he won the coveted Charles Loring Elliot Silver Medal for his drawing from the antique. Since one of the two teachers of the antique at the time was the Danish immigrant artist Emil Carlsen (1853–1932), he probably worked under him. It is tempting to think that Norstad may also have studied painting with Carlson because that would explain the delicate color and light brushwork in *City on a Hill*.

In 1911 Norstad is listed as an artist in the St. Paul City Directory and by the following year as an employee at the Pioneer Company, of which H.H. Bigelow was president. In 1914 he joined Buckbee Mears, where he remained except for 1916 and 1918 when he was apparently a free-lancer. For a time around 1914 he and his new wife Lillian Rosland, a Swedish-American from Red Wing but studying art in St. Paul, were in Glacier Park where he painted promotional pictures for W. Hill of the Great Northern Railroad at the invitation of Louis W. Hill.

Norstad was active in the Twin Cities art world, exhibiting at all the first four annual exhibitions of Works by Northwestern Artists at the St. Paul Institute, 1915–18, and at the State Art Society (later Commission) exhibitions in 1913–14, 16–17. In addition to the awards for *City on a Hill* in 1917, Norstad the same year won first prize on a group of four paintings at the State Art Society Exhibition, where he had the previous year received a Special Mention of the Jury. In 1913 he was admitted to the exclusive professional artists' organization, the Attic Club of Minneapolis, leading to their abandoning the requirement of Minneapolis residency for members.

Norstad left for New York in 1919, where he is registered for two months at the Art Students League in the summer of 1921 but already living in Valhalla, New York, where he remained until moving to California shortly after World War II. During this period he did freelance work from his commercial art studio in New York City to which he commuted by train. Posters were important in his production, and he did work for *The Redbook*. Easel painting diminished in the mid twenties when he began designing and building a house largely of stone and largely with his own hands. He did, however, exhibit four works with the Society of Scandinavian Artists at the Brooklyn Museum in February, 1926. At the 1925 Norse-American Centennial Exhibition in St. Paul he was represented only by two paintings borrowed from Twin Cities collections. Before leaving for California, where he died in Oak Glen, 1962, he burned a good number of his canvases because of storage and moving problems. The family is now aware of only about a dozen extant paintings. In California, building houses continued to take precedence over painting.

Easel painting had been Norstad's love and commercial art his living. In a letter to Louis W. Hill November 4, 1917, he says if he only had $2,000 he would "perpetuate the city of St. Paul with canvas and paint and make a showing down East... Well Mr. Hill, I'm sure going to get there and make good sooner or later." Hill couldn't have taken the hint. Norstad got east but he had probably meant more by "going to get there." Some disillusionment could have been present when at just past sixty he destroyed a fair part of his remaining production.

CARL K. OLDEREN 1879–1959
Illustrations 26, 35

No established artist of Norwegian background kept a lower profile than Carl Olderen though he was among the most refined and sensitive of them. As far as is known, he never sold a painting, beating Van Gogh by one. The reason must have been the low key nature of his work as well as of his personality. Colors are often subdued and harmonious and the compositions balanced and restful. Curiously enough the opposite had led to the same result for his Dutch predecessor. Such is the way of art.

The merit of Olderen's work did not pass totally unrecognized because it was accepted in all the exhibitions easily available to Minnesota artists in the 1920s and 1930s: those at the Minneapolis Institute of Arts in 1923, 28, 30–31, 34, and 39; the State Fair in 1924–28, and 31; and the spring salons of the Woman's Club of Minneapolis in 1935 (perhaps more). It was also accepted in all exhibitions in the region especially for artists of Scandinavian background: those at the Chicago Norwegian Club (six times), the one at the Odin Club of Minneapolis in 1924, and the national one at the 1925 Norse-American Centennial celebration on the State Fair grounds in St. Paul. Occasional comments in the press also occurred, such as mention of two Olderens at the Chicago Norwegian Club exhibition of 1926 which was visited by the Queen of Romania and an observation by John K. Sherman of Minneapolis on a "Pissarro-like" quality in *Washington Avenue Bridge* at the Woman's Club in 1935. On the basis of most of Olderen's work, that would seem out of line, but a painting of Hennepin Avenue in private possession does indeed have such a quality.

Olderen was born October 17, 1879, in Tromsø, a city in that northern area of Norway to which many of our artists trace their background. He emigrated in 1899, probably coming directly to St. Paul where he had relatives. The Minneapolis City Directory of 1906 has him studying at the School of Fine Arts. The choice of institution was natural because his uncle, the prominent stained glass designer and producer Robert T. Giles, was teaching his specialty there at the time.

Olderen reported having had some art training in Norway, but his education was ongoing. In 1906 when he was in art school here, he also completed a course in general illustrating given by the International Correspondence School of Scranton, Pennsylvania. Even after having been employed by the decorator F. A. Leekley in 1915, he took a two-year course in interior decoration at Dunwoody Institute, apparently in 1916–17. As late as 1927 he joined a Saturday painting class offered by Dewey Albinson (1898–1971) at the St. Paul School of Art at which Albinson was director. Judging from the tone of a letter from Albinson to Olderen, the two were friends. It was probably Albinson who drew his attention to the squatters' settlements, of which he had done a painting in the Albinson style two years before his *River Flats in Winter* (Ill. 35) of 1930.

Olderen had to paint houses when decorating jobs were few. But he did not join the federal art programs that from 1933 into the 1940s allowed artists to keep making art through the depression. This may have smacked too much of relief, something that proud Norwegian immigrants found very hard to accept. This was unfortunate not only from an economic standpoint but because it kept him from the interchange between artists that occurred in these programs, something that Syd Fossum found very important. It could also have added to Olderen's visibility.

Olderen lived to be 79, dying on March 24, 1959, but he does not appear to have exhibited after 1939. From the mid forties his major production was small watercolors, primarily of Paris, a city with which he had a vicarious obsession. While Cezanne had been his strongest early influence, Utrillo (1883–1955), whose work he occasionally copied, now became the ideal. Late in 1945 his son Bernard was on the USS Navy cruiser *Indianapolis* that took the atomic materials used in bombing Hiroshima to Tinian. On its way to Guam it was attacked and sunk. After that Olderen packed many of his paintings, notebooks, sketches, and the like in a crate that he nailed shut and put in a dark corner of the basement. In the mid 1990s, his son Arling opened the crate and found that the core of his father's art production had been sealed away for almost fifty years. In bringing three of the paintings to a clinic at the Minneapolis Institute of Arts, he met Mary D. McElroy Bass, whose research has made this presentation of Olderen's story possible.

CYRUS RUNNING 1913–1976
Illustration 34

Running shares with Maakestad a background in what I call a church-related Norwegian-American elite. He was born in Veblen, South Dakota, to the Reverend Alfred Running and Sophia Olsen Running, both of whom were born in America but with roots going back to the Trondheim and Nordfjord area in north central Norway. A reason for the sophistication that sets immigrant pastors' children somewhat apart is not only that they were generally brought up with books and music but that they often had lived in several places. Running had his grade school education in Montana and Idaho and his high school from 1926 to 1930 in Zumbrota, Minnesota, only twenty miles from Rochester, where the fifteen year younger Maakestad would spend his childhood. Both went to St. Olaf College where they got their B.A. degrees. The strong art department that Maakestad found was not yet there for Running so he majored in history and biology.

Indicative of the cultural presence in Reverend Running's home is the fact that all his children, five boys, went into art or music. Orville established the art department at Luther College, Decorah, Iowa, and Paul became a professor of art at Bowling Green University, Ohio. Cyrus also married an artist, Eldred Thorpe, with a background much like his own but from Minneapolis. They met at St. Olaf College and again at the Yale School of Fine Art, where Cyrus studied for about two years. They did not marry until he had received his MFA in 1940 from the University of Iowa, where he had studied with Grant Wood. Iowa was for a time the mecca for art students from what I am calling the Norwegian immigrant elite. Maakestad's artist son Tom told me that he heard a professor from there say in a public presentation some years ago that the University did not want any more sons and daughters of Norwegian clergy in their art department. They had apparently had enough and wanted to change their image.

The year of his graduation, Running was hired to head the art department at Concordia College in Moorhead, a sister institution of St. Olaf College, where Maakestad would go after graduating from Iowa sixteen years later. Running remained in his position until he retired in 1974. Two years later he died on Christmas Day.

Running was an exceptional teacher and leader in addition to being a most prolific and well-received artist. He exhibited at the Minnesota State Fair in 1942, 44, 58, 61, 64, and 68; at the biennial exhibitions of the Minneapolis Institute of Art 1959 and 61; at those sponsored by the Walker Art Center 1947, 49, 56, and 62; and at the Red River annual art exhibitions 1960–63, 65, and 67. In 1958 he was also invited to exhibit four works at the Walker. Beyond this he had by 1970 carried out sixteen large architectural commissions, murals in several media, mosaics, etc. Related to his architectural work was his creation and execution with student help of the backdrops for the Concordia Christmas concerts, a project which he carried out for thirty years and for which he received much praise from the community.

One can not help but compare two artists with Running: Maakestad because of similar background, education, and position, and Beck because of his exceptionally close student/teacher relationship with Running. The three as products of Norwegian-Lutheran colleges who got their advanced training at the University of Iowa do represent a common segment in Minnesota art, probably the most genuinely local in the state. It is characterized by sound craftsmanship and clarity of form. A tendency toward stylization is evident early in their work and gets support from Indian art, both Mexican and American, and in the case of Running, occasionally from Cubism. He and Maakestad can approach total abstraction, but some relation to nature or man remains important.

The above is what the three artists share; beyond that there are also differences. Maakestad and Beck are rooted in nature, the latter exploring the expressive possibilities of its external forms and the former the internal energies that drive it. Running's concentration is on people and their creations. Architecture ranks high in his work, and he often sets up a dialogue between people and their self-defined spaces. Beneath this one feels a deep concern with the human condition, but Running has too much taste, dignity, and fundamental optimism to let that concern override the aesthetic in his work.

AXEL EUGENE SCHAR 1888–1984
Illustration 20

Schar seems from another planet or at least another century. He was born April 12, 1888, as the twelfth child in his Christiania (Oslo), Norway, family. One can understand his need to emigrate at seventeen. His last name came from an ammunition factory, "Skars Krutverk," at which his father worked. Axel had seven children of his own before 1943 when his wife left him in Duluth to join them in California. The couple had by then already celebrated a 34th wedding anniversary, and he would celebrate another 36th such anniversary with a second wife in Worthington, Minnesota, before he died at 96 on November 17, 1984.

During most of his first seventy years Schar had two simultaneous professions, one as a photographer, reporter, and designer, first for the *Duluth Herald* and later for *The Worthington Daily Globe*, and the other as a painter and art teacher. He continued painting until he was 93 and had his last exhibition at the Nobles County Art Center, which he years earlier had helped found. His late work, according to a review by Jim Vante in *The Worthington Daily Globe*, December 30, 1983, presented "entirely new directions—even bolder use of color and design elements, non-objective studies, an artistic explosion of new ideas."

Information on Schar is fairly extensive but vague and sometimes contradictory. Little specific is known from the time of his arrival in America shortly after the turn of the century until he joined the *Duluth Herald*, perhaps around 1920. He supposedly came to an uncle in Ada, Minnesota, and worked for an American newspaper there and later for a Norwegian paper in nearby Crookston. The period also included work on the railroad and as a cook in lumber camps. An amusing contradiction is that he reports employment in a Duluth mission with thoughts of becoming a missionary but was considered "quite cynical at times—and even irreverent" by one of his small-town early students. He could apparently be loose in giving information about himself, understandable considering how much he had to remember. His birth year is recorded both as 1887 and 1888 and his age on arriving in America both as seventeen and twenty. For our purpose the most significant problem is that *Who's Who in Art* has him studying with the Norwegian Frits Thaulow, mentioned nowhere else, and

a funeral bulletin as having "an Art Student Degree" from New York, also not mentioned elsewhere. The former seems unlikely and the latter has not been confirmed.

Whatever Schar's art education, he felt ready to exhibit shortly after joining the *Duluth Herald*, participating in the Scandinavian Artists Exhibition at the Odin Club of Minneapolis in the spring of 1924 with two works, *April Day* and *Breaking of Winter,* and again in 1925 at the Norse-American Centennial exhibition on the fairgrounds in St. Paul with *Norway Pines*. After having tested the ground with his own people, he exhibited at the regular State Fair exhibitions in 1926, 28, 31–32, 39, and 50, sometimes in group exhibitions from Duluth or Worthington. In 1931 he was also in the Arrowhead Art Exhibition at the Duluth Art Institute, an institution he had helped revive. Marine subjects dominated during his Duluth period.

Schar was an institution in himself, founding or revitalizing art organizations and teaching extensively for essentially a lifetime each in two Minnesota communities, Duluth, ca. 1920–45, and Worthington, 1945–84. In 1960 he was also invited to give art a boost in Hibbing. During the 1930s he was involved with the WPA art program in Duluth and at the time also founded the Duluth Camera Club, which still exists. In Worthington he founded the Brush and Pencil Club, which played centrally in the art life of the area. He was highly regarded as a teacher and is said to have launched the careers of William Norman and his wife Sally, Duluth artists who did fine work in the 1930s and 1940s.

Schar was equally adept in oils and watercolors and could paint large, as in the mural panel *Logging Drive on River* (Ill. 20), or quite small, as in some of his watercolor seascapes. These are among his finest and most sensitive works. His Minnesota landscapes can be painted with great detail, as is much Minnesota wildlife art, with which it has some similarities; or they can, like the logging scene mentioned, be broadly executed with an air of freshness and spontaneity. With reference to the former style, it is revealing that he used to tell his students, it takes two people to paint, the artist and someone to tell him when to stop.

J. THEODORE SOHNER 1906–1962
Illustrations 45–46

A man bigger than life, Theodore Sohner (Dahlquist before 1931) was partly victimized by his own abilities. In addition to a varied and extensive production as a painter, he was a singer who between 1933 and 1944 performed eight major roles with the St. Paul Civic Opera and that of Count Almaviva in Rossini's *Barber of Seville* on the road with the American Opera Company. He appeared as a soloist in numerous oratorios and made concert appearances constantly from the twenties to his late years. In 1938 he took a three-year break from his Twin Cities activities and moved with his wife Claudia to New York where he had managers that kept him on a stringent schedule of performing throughout the northeast with but little return after management was paid. His music career took a lighter turn in the mid 1940s when he joined the Lions Club quartet that sang over the entire country and won first place awards in five international competitions. It was performing with the quartet that made him realize his double life was putting too much strain on his heart. He left the group in 1950 but continued other performing and painted incessantly until he was struck by a heart attack November 27, 1962.

The music activities never seemed to reduce Sohner's involvement with art. In both areas he had the support of the family. Music was in the home from the beginning because both his father's and mother's families were heavily involved in it, primarily as related to the church. His father, Jacob Dahlquist (a name often taken for Swedish) was born in Arendal in southern Norway to a family from near Moss with a farm named "Såner," the one that the artist took in anglicized form. The mother was of the prominent land-owning Fyhrie family north of Oslo but was born in Red Wing, Minnesota. They had moved to St. Paul before she married Jacob, and it was here the artist was born March 18, 1906. Music lessons came first, but at the recommendation of his teachers, the boy was entered in an adult art class already at age seven. By the time he went to Johnson High School, he was ready both to sing in and design the sets for the operettas. His cousin-biographer, Ione Brack Kadden (Ill. 46), says that people would tell him either to concentrate on music and give up art or vice versa. "He could do neither," she said, "Both were compulsions not to be denied."

Sohner had a substantial career in art aside from that in music. After taking courses at the St. Paul and Minneapolis schools of art under Dewey Albinson, Cameron Booth, Anthony Angarola (1893–1929), and others, he was by the end of the decade teaching at the St. Paul school. In 1933 he studied for a period with André L'Hote (1885–1962) in Paris. He exhibited constantly, showing at the State Fair in 1930, 33, 35, 42, 44, and 47–52 (four times by invitation); the Minneapolis Institute of Arts exhibitions in 1931, 33–36, 42–47, 51–52, and 62; The Golden Rule Exhibition in 1957; and even the first Red River Annual in 1960. In 1938 he exhibited with the Society of Scandinavian Artists in the Brooklyn Museum. He also arranged one-man showings in several locations and was invited to exhibit at the Barbizon Plaza Hotel Gallery in New York. This got favorable reviews by all the major New York papers. He received first prizes in oils at the State Fair in 1933 and at the Minneapolis Institute of Arts in 1943 and 1951. He also received a second prize in painting at the State Fair in 1944 and a number of lesser awards.

After painting a self-portrait in about 1926 and one of his cousin Ione Brack (Ill. 46) and her mother (Ill. 45) in 1928 and 1930 respectively, portraiture acquired a place in Sohner's production. He did three governors and other officials for the state and several prominent figures for the University. The one of physicist Alfred O.C. Nier done in 1955 is the most relaxed and natural. The male portraits are generally surpassed by the female, which includes several of the Negro actress Vinette Justin Carroll.

I mentioned Sohner becoming a victim of his own abilities. His juggling of two careers prevented the sound, systematic development in either necessary for getting to the very top. As a painter he was uneven, with the finest work being of the family or unpretentious oil sketches of simple streets or shacks in the country. He was superb at woodcuts but did few. He is best when trying least, an indication that he was an artist of considerable natural talent which could be thwarted by pressure.

PETER TEIGEN 1895–1936
Illustration 47

One of the most illustrous of Minnesota artists with Norwegian background, Peter Teigen (both Carl Peterson and Carl Teigen in early years) is also one of the least known. This is partly because he left the area on receiving a B.A. from the University in 1916 and because of his early death. While here, however, he left a mark by doing some highly sophisticated graphics for the *Minnesota Daily* and promotional material for several University functions. These may have contributed to his being elected upon graduating to the Honorary Senior Society for services to the institution. After leaving he exhibited in the Twin Cities twice: first with three mountain scenes from Switzerland and Peru and a portrait at the 1922 Annual Exhibition of Works by Local Artists, Minneapolis Institute of Arts, and again in 1925 at the Norse-American Centennial Art Exhibition in St. Paul with two watercolor scenes from Capri and Tunis and an oil, *Lady of the Frisia*, which won the second award in painting at this national event.

Though ultimately lost to the local and immigrant communities, Teigen had deep roots in them. His father, James (originally Ingebret) Teigen, came in 1869 from Selbu, Trøndelag, Norway, and his mother, Andrine Olson, from Nannestad parish in the same area. They were married in LaCrosse, Wisconsin, in 1878 but moved to the Norwegian settlement of north Minneapolis four years later. Here the father ran a liquor business and here the artist was born on August 28, 1895. Here, too, in a room above the liquor store just seven months earlier, the major Norwegian fraternal organization, the Sons of Norway, was born with James Peterson as one of its founders.

The boy skyrocketed like the organization, but they went different directions. Immediately on graduating from the University, Carl, who in two years would become Peter, entered Harvard and by 1919 had a Master of Architecture degree in spite of also serving some time in the young United States Air Force toward the end of World War I. He had twice held the Shelden Scholarship, and was after graduation invited to travel for two years in Europe, Morocco, and South America with Dr. Denman Ross, a noted authority on art theory and painting techniques. On returning in 1921 he was given an assistantship in fine arts at Harvard. Within

a year, this was broken off by his being granted the coveted Robert Bacon Fellowship for painting, which gave him two more years of study in Europe.

Jobs came as easily as financial support. In 1927, after painting for several years in his own studio, he accepted an assistant professorship at Smith College and a year later the same position at Princeton. This, in 1931, was made an associate professorship. The rocket suddenly nosedived when he died at age 41 on August 13, 1936, at Glenveagh Castle, County Donegal, Ireland, where he was a guest of former Princeton professor Arthur Kingsley Porter's widow. He had sporadically experienced health problems, but the death came as a surprise to many and remains something of a mystery.

Teigen's painting reveals extraordinary competence. He had one-man exhibitions at least in Boston, New York, Philadelphia, and several times at Princeton, the last there being a memorial exhibition two months after his death of works found in his apartment. Those not sold were shipped to Minneapolis and ultimately sold from his sisters' estates. Shortly before his death, Teigen was selected by the Carnegie Institute for inclusion in an exhibition of United States art to be circulated in Canada.

Teigen's subjects ranged from sun-drenched exteriors, to interiors with softly modulated light (Ill. 47), to eerie Irish peat bogs with strangely haunting piles of cut turf. He moved easily between water colors and oils, and during the last year of his life explored the musculature of the male body in a series of both intimate and monumental chalk drawings.

Teigen's notes on art reveal absolute brilliance. In spite of outwardly traditional qualities in much of his known work, his approach was modern. He looked on art as the product of ideas, with subject matter merely the substantiation of them. "Draw only what fits the idea," he says. "Subject is irrelevant. Pure art like music has a tremendous significance of its own." He defended the modern in an exhibit and promoted film as art at Princeton. Teigen appears to have been on his way to great prominence in the art world when he was prematurely struck down.

CHARLES THORESEN 1865–1910
Illustrations 11, the inside covers, and pages 4, 26, 28

No existing major work by Charles Thoresen is known. Why then make the effort of reconstructing the man? It is because the quality of what does exist warrants his being on public record. The only known bodies of material by him are 1) several small sketches in oils and water colors, and numerous pencil drawings, mostly in two sketchbooks passed down through descendants of his wife from a second marriage in Frazee, Minnesota, and 2) a small collection of paintings that went after Thoresen's death in Minneapolis, February 22, 1910, to his younger sister Jorgine (Mrs. Otto Holter) in Bismarck, North Dakota, and have remained with descendants now in Alaska. Much of the original body of work in this latter group is said to be lost.

Charles (originally Karl) appears to have emigrated in 1882 separately from his family, who also came. Although there are contradictions in the records, he was probably born in Spydberg outside Christiania (Oslo) in 1865. He appears as a painter in the Minneapolis City Directory for 1885–86. Here he remains with only a few short breaks, including a stay in Butte, Montana, until his death. He married a Mathilda of Norwegian birth about the time he settled in Minneapolis. He had two sons who because of mental deficiencies did not carry down material from the father's estate.

Thoresen changed his registration from painter to "fresco painter" in 1886–87 when he was 21, and to artist in 1890. From 1893 he is again listed as a painter. He must have had some training in Norway because already in 1886 he had two works, *Spinning* and *The Old Bachelor's Quiet Hour,* in the art division of the First Minneapolis Industrial Exposition. He showed again at the Exposition of 1888 with *Apple Girl.* The titles bring to mind Knud Bergslien, who was the man who conducted the main art school in Oslo during the eighties and who could have been Thoresen's teacher. Since there is no record of further exhibiting, he may have come with the intent of being an artist but, like others, turned to decorating for survival.

Thoresen's education may have gotten a boost in 1888–89. One of his sketchbooks has four pages with dates from between October 9 and 11, 1889, signed "Paris." Since one has details from an interior with notes on the colors, he may have been studying interior decoration there. At any rate, exhibiting now ends and he is a decorator.

Thoresen appears to move between freelancing and affiliation with other decorators. In 1890 he is for a year with L.A. Thiel. In 1896 he joins John B. Berentsen to form Berentsen and Thoresen, which has a separate ad of some size in the Directory. This too lasts only a year and he is on his own until 1905 when he joins Harry B. Cramer Company. It did house and sign painting as well as decorating and also included M.J. Cramer and Wm. A. Marr. Drawings from the fall of 1909 indicate that he remained active and operating at top level until five months before his death, now again apparently on his own.

Thoresen's talent was divided between the precise and objective observation and depiction of nature, even in its broader aspects, and the creation of ornament. About 85 percent of his sketches relate to the latter, but many of the remaining are close-up studies of nature or landscapes and cityscapes that are site-specific. Other than those from Paris, the identified drawings are from Chippewa Falls, Wisconsin (April 1900); Duluth (June 1890), where he even names the streets (Ill. 30); and St. Joseph, Missouri (February 1891). A view of Yosemite Falls from 1909 may not have been done on location.

In his early period the distinction between decoration and free drawing is very clear, with most of the ornament coming from the Baroque and Rococo. The landscapes and cityscapes are totally unembellished presentations of everyday places with remarkably natural perspective and atmosphere. After the turn of the century, the two approaches seem to have merged. Nature is looked at more closely, exemplified by a squirrel in an oak tree (p. 28), but it is given a quality that verges on ornament. Occasionally it can take on an Art Nouveau or Jugend character.

If Thoresen would have used his naturalistic landscape and cityscape drawings as the basis for oils, which he did in a small painting preserved with his sketches (Ill. 11), he would have rated with the best of his time. The public was not ready to support this.

ORABEL THORTVEDT 1896–1983
Illustrations 12–15

A full biography should be written of Orabel, a woman born September 16, 1896, on a farm near Glyndon in northwest Minnesota, who managed to develop in accordance with her personal goals. They were not lofty but quite out of line with what was expected of Norwegian-American farm women. One was to paint animals and the other to memorialize her grandfather Ola Thortveidt (later Thortvedt) and the caravan he led from Houston county in southeastern Minnesota to a spot along the Buffalo River that was something of an oasis on the prairie east of Moorhead.

The blood in Orabel's veins was not common. That grandfather and many in his group came from Fyresdal in Telemark, an area with a highly developed folk culture like that of Seljord in the same province from where Margit Mindrum's father came. The people from there and several other comparable areas constituted, as mentioned in connection with Mindrum, something of an elite, even in the rural immigrant culture. This was totally distinct from the church-related elite with its urban orientation. Books had found their way into the homes of the folk elite as well. The Thortvedt household was very literate. Orabel's father Levi had written in fine lucid prose the story of the trek north which he had experienced as a ten-year old. It was published in many installments in the *Moorhead Daily News* during the early months of 1938. Orabel was then 42. When she began doing oral history and other research to fill out the story and give it the form of a novel, she was merely continuing family tradition. Her version too was published in over thirty installments in the *Moorhead Daily News* during the summer of 1974. Something new to family tradition was the many quaint but well-researched and aesthetically pleasing small watercolors to illustrate the story. These have never been reproduced.

Subjects from her family history, as seen in the powerful portrait of the grandfather with a painting of Houston county behind him (Ill. 13) and ink drawings of his trek north published in the *Warren Sheaf* December 1970 (Ill. 15), represent only one phase of her production. According to John K. Sherman, who reviewed a showing of Orabel's animal paintings in 1934, "this little girl [she was 38] paints nothing else, and wants to paint nothing else."

Animal portraits were her breakthrough in art. The exhibition Sherman commented on was at the State Fair where she by invitation that year showed thirteen animal pastels from her own and four private collections. "An incipient Rosa Bonheur of Minneapolis, perhaps," said Sherman. The analogy stuck. A major article on Orabel by Joan Clifford in *The Gopher* (Minneapolis Athletic Club), April, 1938, was entitled "A Minnesota Rosa Bonheur."

Orabel as an artist is the product of innate talent, intense drive, family support, and to a degree, like Aalbu, Sr., and August Klagstad, a handicap. She was very short and she became close to deaf in her late teens. Her parents encouraged her to study art. She was reluctant to leave the farm where all the animals had names and were her friends, but she told Clifford, "My parents were more farsighted than I was." She got a re-education scholarship that gave her both a lip-reading course and a year of study at the Minneapolis School of Art. This scholarship was renewed twice. She also took work at the University where President L.D. Coffman remarked favorably on her writing ability. She had already begun work on her novel.

For several years in the 1930s Orabel had a successful studio on Ridgewood Avenue, Minneapolis, from which she did portraits of pets and horses for many of the area's most distinguished families. Ultimately love of the farm and her family with its epic history drew her back to Glyndon, where she lived with other unmarried siblings, finally only two sisters, collecting historic information and recording family history in paint and words. She also carried out ambitious projects in restoration and historic preservation on the farm, always assisted by her family. She died at 87 in early November, 1983.

There would have to be a streak of romanticism in someone feeling this close to animals and her family history, but in many ways Orabel was a realist concerned with the actual rather than the imagined, and she was a doer rather than a dreamer. She did not, like many immigrants, feel inclined to create an ideal image of Norway, her ultimate place of origin. Her interest was in gaining detailed and accurate knowledge of her immediate past here in the United States.

MATHIAS (MATT) WOLDEN 1880–1963
Illustrations 23 and page 2

While many of our artists had low profiles, none was as low as Wolden's. There is no written record of him other than vital statistics in official sources and the appearance of his name in exhibition catalogues. Of physical documents there are about four paintings, a sketchbook (p. 2), and a photograph in the Tweed Museum of Art, University of Minnesota, Duluth, and several small oil sketches at Vesterheim, Decorah, Iowa.

Wolden's life here is being reconstructed from the above and the recollections of another artist, Gendron Jensen, who accidentally passed his door at St. Mary's Hospital, Duluth, in 1963 and was told by the nurse, "Here is an artist like you, who is dying." By sheer accident Jensen as a poor art student soon after got a small back room in a rental complex which proved to be Matt Wolden's last residence. Everything indicated it was the man to whom the nurse referred. In the basement were still some of his belongings, which Jensen salvaged and got eventually into the hands of the Tweed Museum and Vesterheim. Of almost equal importance for us are the things the elderly women living in the complex told about Wolden and which Jensen has remembered in great detail these 35 years.

Wolden was born to Johan Olsen and Oline Kristiansdatter on Volden, Østre Gausdal, Gudbrandsdalen, Norway, March 10, 1880. In 1900 he was a keeper of the horses at Haug, a farm in the same area, but left for America aboard the *SS Ultonia* late in 1901. By 1920 he is in Duluth at Hotel Liberty but later at other addresses. Genealogist Lee Rokke obtained the above information.

Wolden was an unmarried, gentle, dignified, well groomed man who was especially kind to children. A circumstance that may have kept him somewhat outside society was insecurity with English. At some point he was picked up on the dock as a day laborer by a small contractor whose name was Bjornnes and who knew Norwegian. On discovering Wolden's intelligence, Bjornnes would occasionally use him for book work, but he was generally a caretaker and handyman in the buildings his employer owned. Bjornnes died, possibly in the 1950s, as did the Swedish painter Knute Heldner (1877–1952), who appears to have been Wolden's mentor, leaving him destitute in his last years, probably a ward of the state.

Painting was apparently what gave purpose to Wolden's life. Being a farm hand at twenty just before emigrating, he probably had no formal art training in Norway. He may, however, have had some exposure to the colony of painters in nearby Lillehammer. What he did during his first twenty years in America is not known, but there must have been involvement with art because he is listed in the American Art Annual of 1923–24. This is just when he is first known to have exhibited. His *The Brook* and *April Snow* were in the Exhibition of Work by Scandinavian Artists at the Odin Club in Minneapolis in 1924, and *The Brook* appeared again that year at the Norwegian Club annual exhibition in Chicago together with *The Spring Tide*. In 1925 he participated in the Norse-American Centennial Exhibition in St. Paul and had two works in the Chicago exhibitions again in 1926 and 27 and one work in 1930. He exhibited twice at the Minnesota State Fair, 1932 and 39, both times in special exhibitions that were invited from artists in the Arrowhead region.

It may be significant that Wolden's first appearance at the State Fair coincided with a special invitational showing of Knute Heldner there. One wonders if he may not have been responsible for getting Wolden to exhibit. This was the first time outside his ethnic group. Wolden may actually be pretty much the product of Heldner's tutelage. A softness in both his color and his brushwork make this seem possible. *Meadow in Bloom* (Ill. 23) is typical, but the brushwork becomes bolder in the larger works. A connection with Heldner was remembered by those who knew Wolden and is suggested by the Wolden sketchbook at the Tweed Museum. It has street scenes from New Orleans where Heldner spent at least winters during much of his mature life. A Whistleresque quality in a very blue ship in dock at night, also at the Tweed, suggests that another Duluth Swede, David Erikson (1869–1946), could also have had some significance for Wolden.

Whatever the influences might be, there is a lyrical quality in Wolden's work that is very much his own. Fortunately the photograph at the Tweed shows fourteen Wolden paintings which give an overview of his production. Except for two portraits, they are landscapes of an airy and open character.

Sources

AALBU, JR., A carefully prepared response in writing to questions submitted by the author, Nov.1999. Exhibition catalogues and file information in MPL-SP.

AALBU, SR.: "En Kunstner," *Minneapolis Tidende*, May 5, 1912; an obituary dated January 24, 1926, probably from the same publication; and listings in the Minneapolis City Directory, 1903–1926. Exhibition catalogues, MIA and MHS. Pictures and personal information from artist's sons Olaf Aalbu Jr. and the late Rolf Aalbu and from his daughter-in-law Jeanette Aalbu. Paintings at Vesterheim, obtained through the efforts of Olaf Jr.

ANDERSON: Donald W. Judkins, *john e. anderson: Minnesota Abstractionist*, Mpls: University Art Museum, 1986. Bruce Rubenstein, "Abstract Painter John Anderson," *Twin Cities*, August 1986, 63–66. "Artist John Anderson Dies, Rite Friday," *Battle Lake Review*, June 10, 1971. Catalogues and clippings in the files of MPL-SC and MHS. Telephone interview with artist's widow Elenore Anderson, St. Paul, Spring 1999, and cousin Donald Anderson, Aberdeen, SD, Summer 1999. Norwegian origins researched by Lee Rokke.

BECK: *Charles Beck Retrospective 1942–1986*, Moorhead, MN: Plains Art Museum, 1986. This lists all published sources. Family background obtained from the artist in a telephone interview, spring 1999.

BERGE: Evelyn Burke, "Minnesota Norwegian Artist Holds Two One-Man Shows in Rochester," *Minneapolis Star*, June 10, 1947. Letter from Elmar Berge, Finnø, Norway, to Francis Urban, Mpls, June 19, 1955 (in artist's files MPL-SC). "Elmar Berge, City Painter, Dies at 63," *Minneapolis Tribune*, Mar. 4, 1956. Letter from Esther Peterson, Mpls., to the author, Mar. 25, 1984. "Norwegian-Minnesota Artist Elmar S. Berge (1893–1956)," *Antiques Auction*, Rochester, MN: John Kruesel Auctioneers and Clerking Company, Oct. 1998. Miscellaneous clippings and information in MPL and furnished by Harry and Josefa Andersen, Chicago.

BOECKMANN: Marilyn Boeckmann Anderson, "Carl L. Boeckmann: Norwegian Artist in the New World," *Norwegian-American Studies 28*, Northfield, MN: NAHA, 1979, and the published sources referred to in its notes, especially B.N.Ekstrand, "Manden og maleriet," *Vikværingen*, Mpls., Jan. 17, 1917, pp. 28–31.

DAHL: "Dahl Inspires Dahl," *Minneapolis Journal*, Mar. 13, 1939. "His Dream 'Inspiration' Turns Artist's Failure into Success," *Minneapolis Star*, Oct. 13, 1940. Einar Dahl, "In Favor of Abstract Artists," Letter to the Editor, unidentified clipping in MPL-SC. "Creativity Not Money Talks,"

Minneapolis Star, Apr. 11, 1963. Steve Van Drake, "Former N.E. Man Keeps Busy In Painting, Being Poet, Philosopher," *Minneapolis Argus*, May 15, 1966. Steve Eide, "Robbinsdale Buys Einar Dahl Paintings," *North Hennepin Post*, Aug. 13, 1987. Steve Eide, "Artist's Family has many memories," *North Hennepin Post*, Vol. 75, No. 42 (date not shown). Numerous other clippings in MPL-SC. Interviews with artist's daughter Alice Bobey and granddaughter Jan Kordash and grandson Roger Stene, spring, 1999.

FOSSUM: The Fossum papers in the archives of MHS or copies of material from them in the artists' files of that institution. Also the artists' files of MPL-SC. Geneological information was obtained from Martin Ulvestad, *Nordmaendene i Amerika* II, Mpls., 1907, and personal information from a telephone interview with the artist's niece, Carly Ryman, Aberdeen, SD, Sept. 21, 1999.

GAUSTA: Marion Nelson, "Herbjorn Gausta, Immigrant Artist 1854–1924," *Norvegica-Americana III*, Oslo: Universitetsforlaget, 1971, also sold as a reprint through Vesterheim. Exhibition catalogues in MPL-SC and the libraries of MIA and MHS.

GRINAGER: The exhaustive collection of information compiled from primary material by the artist's late son Mons and made available to the author by the artist's daughter-in-law Viva. Some of this is now in the artist files at Vesterheim. A limited published source is W.H.N., "Alexander Grinager: an Appreciation," *The International Studio*, Mar. 1914, XXIV–XXV.

HANSSEN: A.K. Larssen, "Om en Nordmann," *Western Viking*, Oct. 1966? (date obscured in clipping). Gareth Hiebert, "St. Paulite on Display," *St. Paul Sunday Pioneer Press*, Jun. 16, 1968. A major feature on Hanssen by Janice Krenmeyer, *Seattle Times Rotogravure Magazine*, Sept., 1967, was not available for this study. Telephone conversations with artist's son Nils, Minneapolis, summer 1999.

HERFINDAHL: The most perceptive is Gaelyn Beal, "The Man Who Paints Time," *Sons of Norway Viking*, May, 1986. Oliver Towne, "Albert Lea Honors Herfindahl, a painter who is still painting," *St. Paul Dispatch*, Feb. 10, 1984. Gareth Hiebert, "Artist is at home in Paris as well as Albert Lea," *St. Paul Pioneer Press*, date missing on copy used. For the art work; Lloyd Herfindahl, *Fragments: The Art of Lloyd Herfindahl*, with an introduction by Gareth Hiebert, Albert Lea: Lloyd Herfindahl, 1994.

KLAGSTAD, ARNOLD: Major is Jamie Besso, "August Klagstad: Norwegian-American Artist," with a chronology for Arnold, unpublished student paper written for the author, 1975. Copies in MPL and at Vesterheim. Mary

Swanson, "Arnold N. Klagstad," *American Paintings and Sculpture in the University Art Museum*, Minneapolis: University Art Museum, 1986. "Arnold Klagstad's Oil Is Picked by Famed N. Y. Gallery," *Minneapolis Journal*, Jan. 14, 1940. "Arnold Klagstad, Artist, to Be Buried Thursday," *Minneapolis Tribune*, May 19, 1954.

KLAGSTAD, AUGUST: The definitive source is Jamie Besso. See Arnold Klagstad.

LARSEN: Robert W. Hayes, *Andreas Ruud Larsen*, four typewritten pages based on an interview with Larsen. Letter from Charles J. Connick, Boston, to Mrs. Andreas Larsen, Minneapolis, Jan. 8, 1943. Letter from Athenaeum Librarian (copy unsigned), Minneapolis, to Mrs. Sigrid T. Larsen, Minneapolis, Jan. 7, 1943. All the above and more in MPL-SC. Also Minneapolis city directories and catalogues of annual art exhibitions in MPL, MIA, and MHS.

LUND: Vital statistics searched by Lee Rokke, Mpls. Exhibition catalogues in MPL-SC and MIA.

MAAKESTAD: Mac Gimse, *A Pilgrimage: I'll Tell You Where I'm Going When I Get There*, Northfield: Steensland Art Museum, St. Olaf College, 1994. An interview with the artist Sep. 8, 1999. Slides furnished by the artist.

MELVOLD: Largely unpublished notes and compilations made by Professor Erik Melvold, Oslo, in 1971 and made available to the author by Mrs. Lena Nordstrom of Minneapolis. These include information from *Budstikken*, Feb. 24, 1885, and *The Minneapolis Tribune*, July 24, 1888. Copies at Vesterheim. Early training is covered in "Eckersbergs Malerskole," *Byminner* (Oslo), 3, 1966, 11. Exhibition catalogues at MPL-SC and MHS.

MINDRUM: Marion Nelson: *Three Landsverks: The Art of an Immigrant Family*, Decorah, IA: Vesterheim, 1990. Major sources used for it were the artist's memoirs *No Change My Heart Shall Fear*, published privately by her daughter Frieda Nowland, Janesville, WI, 1974, and a manuscript *Margit Mindrum, Late Artist* prepared by Frieda Nowland and her daughter Naomi, LaCrosse, WI, 1988.

NORSTAD: A paragraph on Norstad in the catalogue of the Second Annual Art Exhibition of the Chicago Norske Klub, 1921. An unidentified clipping in the papers of Alice Hugy with a letter to the editor regarding the 1917 Exhibition of Works by Northwestern Artists, MHS. Letter from Norstad to Louis W. Hill, St. Paul, Nov. 4, 1917, James J. Hill Reference Library. St. Paul City Directory. Exhibition catalogues, MHS. Telephone interviews with Eloise and Charles Harmon, Pleasant Hill, NY, and Erik Norstad, Carte Madera, CA, fall, 1999.

Sources (continued)

OLDEREN: Mary D. McElroy Bass, *Carl K. Olderen: A Twin City Norwegian-American Artist*, a paper submitted to Professor Frances McDonald, Mankato State University, 1996. Further research in the Minneapolis City Directory and interviews with Arling and Lois Olderen, Minneapolis, 1998–99.

RUNNING: Claudia Baker, *Cyrus Running, Artist, Teacher*, Moorhead, MN: Red River Art Center, 1974. This was provided me by Joan Buckley, Moorhead. Exhibition catalogues in MIA, MHS, and MPL-SC. Viewing Running's work at Concordia College with Barbara Anderson of its Art Department.

SCHAR: Gene, *A Memory Sketch of Axel Eugene Larsen (Skar)*, privately published in Worthington. Lew Hudson, "City artist A.E. Schar dies, *Worthington Daily Globe*, Nov. 1984. "A.E. Schar," *Worthington Daily Globe*, Nov. 21, 1984. Biography from Schar funeral bulletin in Nobles County Historical Society. Lee Rokke, Mpls., MN, and Roxanne at the Nobles County Historical Society assisted in the location of the above materials. Exhibition catalogues in MIA, MHS, and MPL-SC.

SOHNER: Ione N. Kadden, *J. Theodore Sohner*, St. Paul: Ione Kadden, 1926. Marion Nelson, *J. Theodore Sohner 1906–1962*, Decorah, IA: Vesterheim, 1986. Exhibition catalogues in MIA, MHS, and MPL-SC.

TEIGEN: An almost definitive collection of the artist's papers in the Vesterheim archives, Decorah, IA, donated by James Billings, Mpls. Of special importance were *Memorial Exhibition of Painting by Peter Teigen*, a single folded sheet. "Professor Peter C. Teigen dies suddenly in Ireland," *The Princeton Herald*, Aug. 21, 1936. "Contemporary American Art on View Analzyzed by Professor Teigen in Interview," *The Daily Princetonian*, Feb. 19, 1929. *Modes of Presentation*, typewritten notecard. "Bortvandret Stifter," *Sønner av Norge*, Mpls., Apr. 1924, father's obituary. Family research by genealogist Lee Rokke.

THORESEN: Two sketchbooks, loose drawings and painted studies, and several photographs made available to me by Rosemari Anderson, Frazee, MN. An undated letter sent to me and others by Mrs. Anderson about 1994 asking for information about Thoresen and stating what was known by the family. Exhibition catalogues at MPL-SC. A telephone interview with Mr. and Mrs. Richard Poor, Douglas, Alaska, Oct. 1999.

THORTVEDT: The vast collection of papers of and related to Orabel made available by Eva and Carl Hedstrom, Anoka, MN, and material furnished by Betty Bergland, River Falls, WI, and James Skree, Houston, MN. Central materials other than those identified in the biography are John K. Sherman, "Art Angles," *Golfer and Sportsman*, Sept., 1934. Doris Eastman, "History Kept Alive By Thortvedt Sisters," *Fargo Forum*, Jun. 17, 1970. "Orabel Thortvedt," a short obituary, *Fargo Forum*, Nov. 2, 1983.

WOLDEN: Telephone conversation with Gendron Jensen, Taos, NM, Dec. 1999. Letter from Patricia Maus, St. Louis County Historical Society, to Carol Hasvold, Decorah, IA, May 21, 1991. Search for vital statistics by Lee Rokke, Mpls. Exhibition catalogues in MPL-SC and MHS.

Selected General Bibliography

Exclusive of material on individual artists covered in the preceding sources of information on them

Accomplishments; Minnesota Art Projects in the Depression Years (an exhibition catalogue). Minneapolis: University of Minnesota Gallery, n.d.

American Paintings and Sculpture in the University Art Museum Collection. Minneapolis: University Art Museum, 1986.

Boe, Roy. *The Development of Art Consciousness in Minneapolis and the Problems of the Indigenous Artist* (an MA thesis). University of Minnesota, 1947.

Coen, Rena. *Minnesota Impressionists*. Afton, MN: Afton Historical Society Press, 1996.

Coen, Rena. *Painting and Sculpture in Minnesota 1820–1914*. Minneapolis: University of Minnesota Press, 1976.

Erickson, Rolf H. "Norwegian-American Artists' Exhibitions Described in Checklists and Catalogs." *Norwegian-American Studies*, vol. 31 (1986), pp 283–304.

Fielding, Mantle. *Dictionary of American Painters, Sculptors and Engravers*, Glenn B. Opitz, ed. Poughkeepsie, NY: Apollo Book, 1986.

Hansen, Carl G.O. *My Minneapolis*. Minneapolis: C.G.O. Hansen, 1956.

Helsell, Charles. *Made in Minnesota I; Art at 3M* (an exhibition catalogue). St. Paul: 3M, 1997.

Lovoll, Odd S. *The Promise of America: A History of the Norwegian-American People*. (Rev. ed.) Minneapolis: University of Minnesota Press, 1999.

Lovoll, Odd S. *The Promise Fulfilled: A Portrait of Norwegian-Americans Today*. Minneapolis: University of Minnesota Press, 1998.

Nelson, Marion J. "Norwegian-American Painting in the Context of the Immigrant Community and American Art." *Nordics in America: The Future of Their Past*, ed. Odd S. Lovoll. Northfield, MN: Norwegian-American Historical Association, 1993, pp. 157–186.

Nelson, Marion J. (with contributions by David Mandel and Darrell Henning). *Norway in America*. Decorah, IA: Vesterheim, 1989.

O'Sullivan, Thomas. "Robert Koehler and Painting in Minnesota, 1890–1915," *Art and Life on the Upper Mississippi, 1890–1915*. Newark, DE: University of Delaware Press, 1994.

Spangler, Kay V. *Survey of Serial Fine Art Exhibitions and Artists in Minnesota, 1900–1970*, I–II. St. Paul: Minnesota Historical Society, 1997.

Swanson, Mary Towley. "Dewey Albinson: The Artist as Chronicler," *Minnesota History*, vol. 52, no. 7, 264–278. St. Paul: Minnesota Historical Society, 1991.

Swanson, Mary Towley. *The Divided Heart: Scandinavian Immigrant Artists 1850–1950* (an exhibition catalogue). Minneapolis: University Gallery, 1982.

Torbert, Donald. *A Century of Art and Architecture in Minnesota*. Minneapolis: University of Minnesota Press, 1958.

Ulvestad, Martin. *Nordmændene I Amerika* II. Minneapolis: Ulvestad, 1907.

Union List of Artist Names, I–IV (published on behalf of the Getty Art History Information Program). New York: G.K. Hall & Co., 1994.

Van Tassell, Katherine. *Minnesota Artists Look Back* (an exhibition catalogue). St. Paul: Minnesota Museum of Art, 1988.

Who's Who in American Art. New Providence, NC: Marquis Who's Who, 1999.

Serials: City directories for Minneapolis and St. Paul and *The Bulletin of the Minneapolis Society of Fine Arts* and its successors.

Catalogues and checklists of Minnesota exhibitions including Minnesota artists and the files on artists in the Minneapolis Public Library Special Collections and the Libraries of the Minneapolis Institute of Arts and the Minnesota Historical Society